DDR-GUIDE

A COMPANION TO THE PERMANENT EXHIBITION

Editor
Quirin Graf Adelmann v. A. and Gordon Freiherr von Godin
Texts
Sören Marotz, Elke Sieber, Dr. Stefan Wolle
Translation
Andrew Smith
Design, typesetting, illustrations
Michaelis Design
Includes texts by: Andreas Menn, Robert Rückel, Kathrin Strohl, Jochen Voit
Publisher
DDR Museum Verlag GmbH, Karl-Liebknecht-Str. 1, 10178 Berlin
Printed
Medialogik, Im Husarenlager 6a, 76187 Karlsruhe
First Edition of July 2017, Printed in Germany

Acknowledgements
Melanie Alperstaedt (copy-editing), Maria Bartholomäus (photographs), bpk-Bildagentur, Bundesarchiv, Bundesbeauftragter für die Unterlagen der Staatssicherheit, Deutsche Fotothek, Julia van Duijvenvoorde (copy-editing English), Agentur Focus, Rebecca Hall (copy-editing English), Albert Hulm, Anett & Stephan Hüssen, Peter Kenzelmann, Jörn Kleinhardt (photographs), Margret Kowalke-Paz (copy-editing), pa picture alliance, Presse- und Informationsamt der Bundesregierung, Robert-Havemann-Gesellschaft, Arthur Schmidt, Harald Schmitt, Felix Schwab, Stiftung Gedenkstätte Berlin-Hohenschönhausen, ullstein bild, Umbruch Bildarchiv and all museum guides, employees of the museum and its donors of objects and supporters.

»DDR Guide – A companion to the permanent exhibition«
ISBN: 978-3-939801-20-7
This publication follows ISBN 978-3-939801-17-7 »GDR-Guide – A Journey to a bygone State«, ISBN 978-3-939801-14-6 »GDR-Guide – Everyday life in a long-gone state in 22 chapters« and ISBN 978-3-939801-01-6 »The GDR Museum – A guide to the permanent exhibition. A hands-on experience of everyday life«

Cover picture: © Sigrid Marotz

DDR-GUIDE

A COMPANION TO THE PERMANENT EXHIBITION

DDR MUSEUM **VERLAG**

FOREWORD

The DDR left the stage of history shortly before its 41st birthday. Singing the German national anthem and watching the fireworks in front of the Reichstag in Berlin, the masses cheered its departure. What exactly had died this night? The first attempt to construct a fair society? An anti-fascist alternative to the revanchist regime established in West Germany? Or a Soviet colony imposed on its population against their will? Even if the latter were true, was not the initial enthusiasm of many of its members a sign of the hope for a better world? Did not the people of East Germany get on with their lives? Were they not perhaps even better off than under the »freedom« of the market economy?

These and other questions have constituted the focus of a long debate which began on that evening in 1990 and continues to this day. The exhibition of the DDR Museum does not claim to provide a conclusive answer to these questions, but it does seek to address them through providing a narrative of the years 1945–1989 with a focus on the everyday life of the DDR as lived by its ordinary inhabitants. Our slogan »A Hand-on Experience of History« does not just refer to the unique level of interaction which our installations provide, but indicates the direction taken by it. Outlining the experience of living under a constant bombardment of propaganda and the shadow of coercion and servility, the exhibition traces the popular perception of and response to this situation and puts the visitor in the shoes of the average East German. How would I have reacted? Would I have done as was expected? What if anything is different about then and now? These are the questions with which each visitor is confronted.

Seeking to compare the experiences of dictatorship and political freedom, we use fascinating exhibits and state-of-the-art installations in order to reproduce the vista of an ordinary life from the cradle to the grave. Placing great importance on accessibility, we use original artefacts and interactivity to explain important topics to all visitors, young and old and both from Germany and abroad.

A private museum without any public funding, we exist on the basis of the admission fee paid by some 600,000 visitors per year. In addition to performing the educative functions of a public museum, we are also present in the Social Media, provide a range of educational services and finance and develop a range of educative games and programmes of academic research. Our collection of over 300,000 historical artefacts represents the largest collection pertaining to DDR history in the world and represents an important conservational undertaking. We also organize new exhibitions in our foyer.

Although this book provides a range of important background information with which to achieve a better understanding of our exhibition, we hope that the reader uses it to learn about life in the DDR and engage with the wider and more significant questions of historical and political importance relevant for our life here and now and the future of our society.

Enjoy a hands-on experience of history!

Quirin Graf Adelmann v. A.   Gordon Freiherr von Godin

CONTENTS

PUBLIC LIFE

PARTY AND STATE

LIFE IN A TOWER BLOCK

END AND NEW BEGINNING

A STATE COMES ...
AND GOES

1

In the beginning was defeat. With the unconditional surrender by the German Empire on 8 May 1945, the close of the Second World War brought the total destruction of its originator. Dividing Germany into four zones of occupation, the victorious allies – the USA, Great Britain, France and the Soviet Union – all set the tone in their own sphere of influence. Despite the initial popularity of a number of Soviet measures (such as a wide-reaching land reform), the Soviet Zone of Occupation soon developed into a Communist dictatorship under the leadership of the Socialist Unity Party of Germany (SED). Founded on 7 October 1949, the German Democratic Republic (DDR) never enjoyed any level of popular consent.

Popular disaffection over poor living conditions and repression culminated in mass strikes and demonstrations on 17 June 1953; only Soviet tanks prevented a revolution. Unhappy at the prevailing conditions, ever-more East Germans (especially the young and well-educated) voted with their feet and fled to West Germany. Alarmed at the prospect of losing his most valuable workers, Walter Ulbricht

2

3

1 FDJ at the mass meeting in Berlin in support of the establishment of the DDR and the election of Wilhelm Pieck to the office of President, 11.10.1949

2 Police and soldiers guard the construction of the Berlin Wall. The operation started on 13.8.1961.

3 Addressing the VIII SED Party Conference, Brezhnev renews his support for the »steadfast alliance« between the Soviet Union and the DDR, 16.6.1971

obtained Soviet permission to seal off the last remaining gap in the Iron Curtain. The building of the Berlin Wall (13 August 1961) left East Germans trapped in the DDR.

Forced to make the best of a changed situation, people set about building themselves a life. The SED leadership sought to help them in their endeavour and set about modernizing society, promising greater prosperity, artistic freedoms and less repression. Nevertheless, wide-spread hopes of achieving »Socialism with a human face« were decisively dashed on 21 August 1968, following the military repression of the Prague Spring in Czechoslovakia.

After the international recognition of the DDR as a state in the 1970s, the SED felt forced to initiate reforms aimed at engineering an apparently more open society. International journalists were granted accreditation, international visitors welcomed and postal and telephone communications were improved. As a counterweight, spending was increased on the security apparatus. A comprehensive programme of social provision launched in a bid to stabilize the system led only to massive debt and the threat of bankruptcy.

1

This situation was compounded by the popular hopes raised in the DDR by Mikhail Gorbachev's programme of reform. The latent crisis of DDR Socialism now became acute, threatening its very existence. With a group of dissidents crystallizing under the protection of the Church, the cry for human rights and freedom became louder. The celebrations to mark the fortieth anniversary of the DDR held in October 1989 were overshadowed by mass demonstrations in Leipzig, Berlin and other large cities. At first, the state reacted slowly to this mass movement, and then surprised everyone by announcing freedom of travel on 9 November 1989. This took effect immediately, and the crowds flocking to the borders resulted in the fall of the Berlin Wall. A peaceful revolution had brought freedom and democracy and eventually the reunification of Germany on 3 October 1990. The DDR had been consigned to history.

GERMAN DEMOCRATIC REPUBLIC (DDR)

- Area 108,333 km^2
- Population: 16,675,000 (1988)
- Population density: 154 per km^2
- Capital: Berlin (East)
- Administrative structure: 14 districts and East Berlin

1 The largest anti-government demonstration in East Germany. Alexanderplatz, East Berlin, 4.11.1989
2 The abandonment of border controls at the border crossing Bornholmer Straße (Bösebrücke) in Berlin at c. 23.30. East Germans flood to the West, 9.11.1989

A DAY IN THE LIFE OF HERR MÜLLER

Responding to the daily summons of the alarm at six o'clock, Herr Müller glares at an unfamiliar reflection in the bathroom mirror. A quick slurp of coffee aids the process of self-recognition and reminds her to eat breakfast on the go. Plunging into the crammed tramcar, she makes her way to work. Whether in West or East, under Capitalism or Communism, this is what everyday life looks like for many people in an industrial society.

Having arrived at work in the office of the HO furniture store »Modernes Wohnen« (Modern Living) Herr Müller lights up the first cigarette of the day. People smoked a lot and at all hours in East Germany. Chatting with her colleagues about the latest murder mystery on television last night, each member of our little group must make a snap judgement: can I trust this person enough to indicate that I was watching West German television? Better not risk it.

Looking at the clock at ten o'clock, Herr Müller decides that her work can wait and turns to some private tasks. She calls the »Kommunale Wohnungsverwaltung«, the centralized letting agency responsible for the majority of flats in East Germany, to make a complaint about the damage to the door on her oven. This is another aspect of everyday life – the small things are important. The telephone rings and rings without answer. A small hand-written sign on the door of the office in which the ringing telephone is sitting informs

1

would-be visitors that Herr Müller is absent and will not be providing any service.

The author of this handwritten sign is on the bus. Having made a number of fruitless telephone inquiries about the likely arrival of her new sofa, she has decided to speak to the unhelpful person who answered her calls. This Herr Müller was rather rude, and fobbed her off every time with some excuse. She has decided to complain. She might even threaten to write to the government to vent her frustration about the poor customer service and slow delivery. This is another important aspect of life under Socialism – nothing ever happens when it is supposed to and people have to expend a lot of energy trying to obtain very little.

1 A new housing estate in Marzahn (Berlin), 1981   2
2 Opening of the new pedestrian precinct »Straße der
Befreiung« (Liberation Road) in Dresden (Innere Neustadt), 1979

Come twelve noon, a rumour goes round the letting agency that fruit is on sale in the shopping centre. Three of the office staff rush off clutching shopping bags and promise Herr Müller to buy her some peaches. This is not an empty promise – the collective always holds together against the vagaries of life. Herr Müller tells her boss that she needs to go to the housing agency. She might even not be able to come back today. The boss is not happy, but lets her go. This is a further aspect of life in East Germany – life is often difficult and people try and help each other.

Herr Müller runs through her options on her way to the housing agency. She will probably need to make a scene. She might even write to the government. At two o'clock she is standing in front of the neat handwritten note on the door informing all and sundry of the absence of Herr Müller. At about the same time, Herr Müller is fuming at the absence of Herr Müller.

Photograph DDR Museum

THE WALL

The images of the Berlin Wall have become etched on the minds of millions: large walls, barbed wire fences, tank traps, a death strip, watch towers. The death trap running through the centre of Berlin since 13 August 1961 involved a lot of different types of barriers, which became known collectively as »The Berlin Wall«. Not just a demarcation line, this barrier represented the foundations of the DDR. More than a mere physical object it was the concrete expression of a political creed. Musing on the »Prussian Icarus«, Wolf Biermann sang:

»The barbed wire becomes intertwined with our heart, growing into our skin reaching into our head and brain. Girding our loins with wire we cut ourselves off from the world...«

Supporters of the Socialist system understood the necessity of the Wall. For them, the deaths on the border were a price worth paying. In truth however, the Wall was a clear admission of moral and political bankruptcy, given expression in the deaths of those whose only crime was a desire to live elsewhere. Retreating to a world of resigned acceptance, East Germans sought to make the best of circumstances. This explains the nostalgia of many East Germans and the impression of stability that contemporary observers noted. A zoo cage certainly protects the lions and tigers from the outside, but it also keeps them from reaching their natural potential. The popular movement of 1989 soon showed that Socialism behind bars was a concept without a future. It also showed how Socialism needed the bars to survive.

A view of a street in the Prenzlauer Berg area from West Berlin, 1985

STRUCTURE OF THE BERLIN WALL

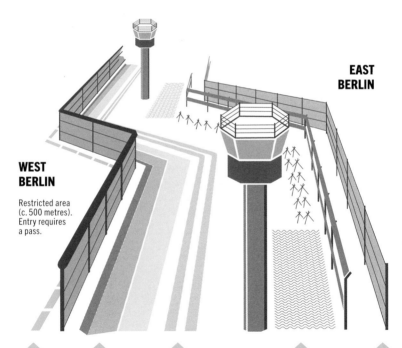

EAST BERLIN

WEST BERLIN

Restricted area
(c. 500 metres).
Entry requires
a pass.

Course of the
border

Vehicle trap

Patrol strip

Death strip and
tank traps

Backland
wall

Wall to the
West

Sand strip

Watch towers

Alarmed
fence

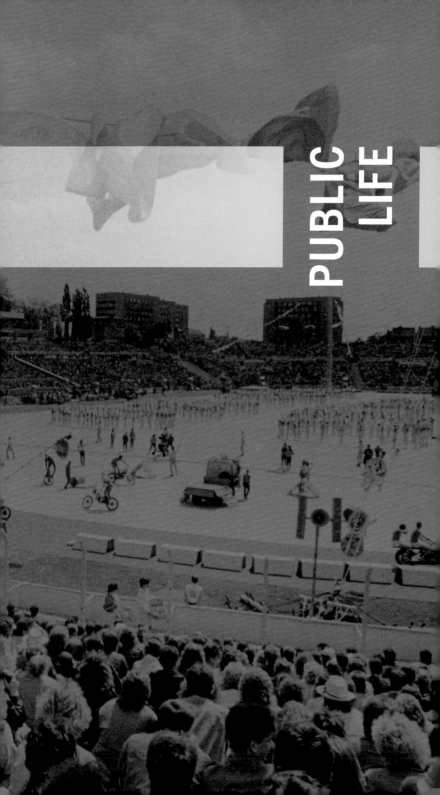

PUBLIC LIFE

The »Schwalbe« – a Swallow – only became popular after its production had ceased. Young East Germans preferred other models of scooter – the »Star« or the »Hawk« – and laughed at the Swallow as being just a little bit uncool. The million or so Swallows made in the DDR were ridden to death by district nurses and telegram boys.

East Germans were allowed to ride a motorized two-wheeler with a maximum engine capacity of 50 cm^3 and a top speed of 60 km/h from the age of 15; this fact alone ensured that scooters or mopeds became very popular. Made by »VEB Fahrzeug- und Jagdwaffenwerk Ernst Thälmann« in Suhl, they cost 1,265.00 DDR Marks.

The Swallow in our exhibition retains its original paintwork as indicated by the original label »technisch überprüft« (inspection passed). With 13,346 km on the clock of this particular exhibit, the model has proven itself to be hard-wearing. The simple construction was easy to repair, and they were often tuned or »souped up« after 1989 to bring them up to the speed of Capitalism.

TECHNICAL DATA

- Date of construction: 1979 (over a million exemplars of the »Swallow« were built between 1964 and 1986)
- Motor: 49.6 cm^3 air-cooled two-stroke motor
- Performance: 3.6 HP
- Top speed: c. 60 km/h
- Consumption: under 3 l/100 km

CARDBOARD COMRADE

1

The mechanisms of the ticket machines for trains and busses had a highly idiosyncratic construction: the coin slot and ticket dispenser were actually constructed separately from each other. The result was that you could pay the 20 Pfennig fare, but it was not entirely necessary. Other methods of transport in the DDR were not free but were still inexpensive. This did not make them reliable. The trains of the »Imperial German Railways« (itself an anachronism in a Socialist society) were dirty and full. A single flake of snow was often sufficient to result in disruptions and cancelled trains due to »extreme weather conditions«. Passengers on the bus and tram networks could tell a similar story. Forty years of minimal investment in the transport system produced a unanimous popular wish: everybody wanted a car.

2

The »Trabi« was not the only car on offer. The Wartburg was manufactured in Eisenach, and Socialist brother states delivered Škodas and Ladas. Nevertheless, the leading figures of the republic preferred the western luxury model Volvo. Despite such variety, the Trabi remained the uncontested symbol of East German mobility. A Russian word meaning »companion«, many Trabis became a trusted friend to their East German owners, first as a dream (waiting times for the car could stretch to 16 years) and then as a status

---

1 Trabis parked in front of a parade of shops in the Erfurt District, 1971
2 Purchase contract for a Trabant 601-S, 1983

Photograph DDR Museum

symbol and a hobby. The construction of this »cardboard box with an engine« was so simple that the happy owner was usually able to repair the majority of faults themselves. Made of Duroplast, a mixture of cotton felt and plastic, the housing was lightweight, rust-free and saved expensive metal. Should the traveller have ambitious plans — such as a trip to Bulgaria — he would be careful to pack the requisite tools and mechanical manuals so as to ensure a safe return. Partly because they required so much attention, the driver often developed a strong and trusting bond with his car. The more committed driver could even buy records about his car such as the famous refrain »A sky blue Trabant, driving through the countryside ...« or tell jokes. One of the best: »what do you call a Trabi on the top of a hill? — A miracle!«

PRIVATE CARS IN THE DDR IN 1988

Trabant (DDR) 1,904,000
Wartburg (DDR) 606,000
Lada (USSR) 329,000
Škoda (ČSSR) 303,000
Moskwitsch (USSR) 127,000
Dacia (Romania) 68,000
Saporoschez (USSR) 56,000
Polski Fiat (Poland) 34,000
VW Golf (FRG) 22,000
Wolga (USSR) 19,000
Mazda (Japan) 11,000
Zastava (Jugoslavia) 5,000
Citroën (France) 2,500
Volvo (Sweden) 1,000

Shopping centre, Nordhausen 1982

queues so as to have something for the future, or just to exchange. Such behaviour produced bizarre situations. Bedclothes were hardly ever available to buy, but the average East German had far more sheets than they would ever need. Many perishable goods were also bought but never eaten and there was considerable waste. The unreliable refuse collection services meant that large piles of rubbish were often left lying about.

29

EVERYDAY CHAOS

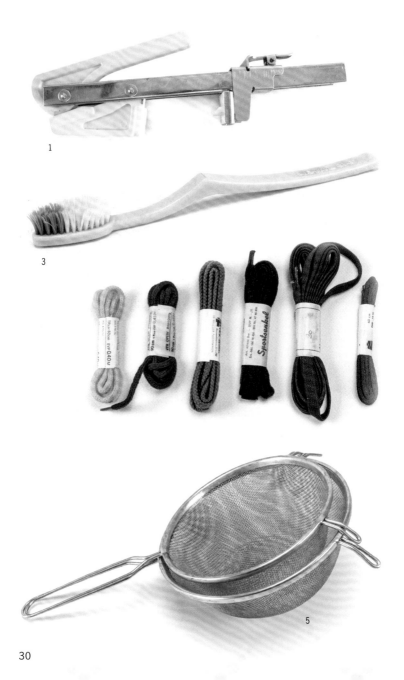

1

3

5

VEB Holz- und Metallwaren
Leutenberg
Fußball-Hupe
Schl.-Nr. 5491300/364/00045
ELN 182 39 130
EVP M -.50

2

4

The hostility of the East German state to private enterprise and the mass closure of many private companies deprived the DDR economy of its most reliable subcontractors. As such, nationalized companies lacked supplies and were forced to produce an uneconomical range of goods. Scissors, bootlaces and nails were made in factories originally intended for bicycles and tie racks, whilst poor central co-ordination resulted in the uneven availability of goods. For example, a paper mill would suddenly start producing tin-openers, unaware that the local toy factory had also made the same decision. The consumer could buy as many tin-openers as they liked, but lacked toys and writing paper. No-one had thought to produce hair pins.

1 Tin opener
2 Klaxon horn
3 Toothbrush
4 Bootlaces
5 Sieve
6 Bottle opener

6

SOLD OUT

East Germans did not suffer particularly acute hardship, but were often hard pressed to find what they were looking for when they wanted it. The most advanced of the Eastern bloc nations, the DDR economy produced goods of international quality. Nevertheless, this fact did not make itself apparent in the shops and shopping centres of East Germany.

One week, letter-writers could not buy paper or envelopes, the next saw an acute shortage of honey or ketchup.

Fruit and vegetables were always scarce, not just exotic fruits but even tomatoes and cucumbers. Meat and cured meat needed for the weekend was best bought on a Thursday. The shortages were the result of the planned economy, inefficient production and a cumbersome bureaucracy. The central allocation of all goods meant that they often did not arrive where they were needed. Some products were rarely seen because they disappeared abroad as

1

exports. Scarcity did not encourage economy; rather it engendered waste. Prices and rents were not fixed according to supply and demand, but were set by the state and often heavily subsidized. Electricity, gas, water and a number of basic foodstuffs were so cheap that people were often overgenerous in their use. The East German shopper resembled a hunter: never leaving the house without a shopping bag, they kept their eyes peeled for spoils. The customers no longer bought what they needed, but what was on offer — people would even join queues without knowing what was being sold. The most commonly heard phrase in a shopping centre was: »sold out«, related in a tone intimating both tiredness and irritation.

1 A queue in front of a bookshop, 1988
2 Shopping centre on Berliner Platz in an Erfurt housing estate, 1975
3 (next page) The children's department of the »Centrum-Warenhaus« on Alexanderplatz (Berlin), 1970

2

KONSUMGENOSSENSCHAFT

Established in 1945, the »Konsumgenossenschaft« set up a chain of shops which reached 35,000 in number by 1980. Predominantly found in rural areas, the organization also included some 6,000 restaurants and over 1,000 factories producing everyday foodstuffs.

»KONSUMENT« DEPARTMENT STORES: A »Konsument-Warenhaus« had been opened in 13 towns and cities by 1988. The phrase »going to the Konsum« became a recognized figure of speech. Customers collected coupons which they could present at the end of the year to qualify for a cash premium.

»KONSUMENT« MAIL ORDER COMPANY: Trousers, shoes, bags, jewelry, radios and furniture were all available from the »Konsument-Versandhaus« based in Karl-Marx-Stadt (Chemnitz). Aimed predominantly at the rural population, shortages meant that the postal sales were stopped in 1976.

»GENEX-VERSANDHANDEL«

The acronym Genex stood for »gifts and small exports« (»Geschenk- and Kleinexporte GmbH«) and represented a company founded in 1956 with the sole aim of generating international income in hard currency. As such, only foreigners could order from the company. West Germans would often purchase televisions, furniture, household appliances and even cars for friends and family in East Germany.

HANDELSORGANISATION

Established in 1948, the »Staatliche Handelsorganisation« was intended as a competitor to the »Konsumgenossenschaft«. Later it was to be found in rural areas only; the »Konsumgenossenschaft« concentrated on sales in towns and cities.

INTERSHOPS: Opened in 1955 as a duty-free shop for western travelers, it acted as a source of foreign currency. After 1974, East Germans could also purchase goods with hard currencies.

»CENTRUM« DEPARTMENT STORES: Opened in the majority of medium-sized and large cities, »Centrum« department stores offered a relatively generous range of consumer durables. The 1970s saw a large building programme – one famous store was to be found on the Alexanderplatz in East Berlin.

»CENTRUM« MAIL ORDER: Opened in 1956, this Leipzig-based mail order company was intended to enable rural customers to purchase more advanced products not otherwise available in their area. It soon became clear however, that city dwellers also used the catalogue service. Shortages made for long delivery times.

»EXQUISIT« AND »DELIKAT« STORES: Opened in 1962 and 1966 respectively, these shops sold high-quality and expensive clothing and foodstuffs. A number of the goods were western imports, others taken from DDR production. The latter step only served to exacerbate existing shortages.

GARDEN PARADISE

Although the working-class allotment keeper was a familiar sight from the mid-19th century onwards, he was a figure of ridicule in the DDR. This was an illogical attitude, for those laughing at the hobby gardeners forgot that they were the only ones to enjoy vegetables and salad on a regular basis. Gardeners could also hand over their produce to the state for good cash prices or for payment in kind. The export of fresh fruit and vegetables for much needed hard currency meant that the allotment made an important contribution to the East German economy. By the 1970s, many people actually invested more time and energy in their gardens than in their paid employment; some would even spend their weekdays organizing their weekend gardening

A typical East German weekend home, 1986

activities. The state found this retreat into the private sphere somewhat vexing — after all, people were supposed to enjoy working and living in the collective — but eventually came to accept the practice. Far better that people were pottering about in their gardens than trying to escape to the West.

NATIONALLY-OWNED PRODUCTS

The names of the products on the super-market shelves promised a world of glamour hardly distinguishable from the western advertisements. Bicycles were named »Diamant« (Diamond), wall units »Carat« and a popular brandy went under the name »Goldkrone«. Smokers puffed on »Juwel« (Jewel) cigarettes and all manner of broken implements were fixed with »Duosan rapid« instant glue. The East German economy also offered a whole host of instant products including »Tempo-linsen« (Tempo Lentils), coffee powder »Im Nu« (literally meaning »in a fix«) or even »Ku(rz)Ko(ch)-Reis« (Quick Rice). All this modernity and practicality was designed to make a housewife's life considerably easier.

Despite such promises, consumers watched the adverts on West German television with wide eyes. The highest praise for eastern products — if meant only ironically — was the epithet »just like a western product«. Packets sent from West Germany ensured a steady stream of western consumer goods into the DDR. Initially angered by this western cultural influence, the SED sought to stigmatize it: Western fashion was frowned upon and school teachers reprimanded any of their charges found writing with West German pens or stationary. Even posters of West German pop stars and footballers were confiscated. The later years of the DDR saw a relaxation of attitudes, as it was recognized that this small-scale practice

of private imports served to relieve the hard-pressed DDR retail sector. The East German authorities were happiest if western money was used to buy goods from the »Intershops«. Foreign currency spent in this equivalent of a duty-free shop allowed the purchase of tax-free western goods and with them a little bit of international flair. It was just that they were all terribly expensive.

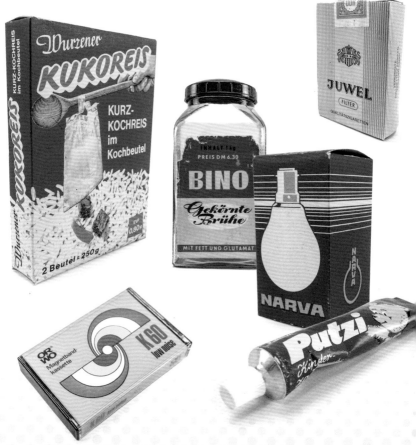

THE HONOUR OF WORKING

1

The DDR was proud to call itself the »Workers' and Peasants' State«. Although the average worker and peasant had little or no influence on politics, the DDR never tired in pointing out the honour involved in getting one's hands dirty. Indeed, every citizen had a job, and the ever-present labour shortage meant that those refusing to work were punished for their antisocial behaviour.

The employer or »company« was much more than a source of work and money, it was also a provider of identity, family support and social services. It provided accommodation, hospitals, childcare, sports clubs, cultural activities and even holidays. The employer sought out bright young workers and recommended them for a place at university; graduates often returned to their employer for a job. The employer even looked after former employees and sent them gifts at Christmas.

2

1 Entrance to a petrochemicals work,
Schwedt an der Oder 1979
2 A family working on the fields,
Birkholz 1982

Many people came to see their job as a second home and it was not unusual that a worker would remain with an employer for his whole life. Colleagues in the »work brigade« were more often than not friends after work, and went out and travelled together. If someone moved house, their colleagues were always on hand to do the carrying and even the redecoration. Often, the materials for repairs and renovations were »borrowed« from the employer. If a worker absented himself from work, his mates would often try to find out why. As such, the collective did actually become the »seed-bed of Socialist society« and a method of social control, whilst also simultaneously functioning as a survival mechanism in a society characterized by shortage.

41

GROSS SALARIES, 1988

899 – 1,275 M

PRODUCTION WORKER (group 4–9)

1,024 – 1,493 M

MASTER CRAFTSMAN (group 8–11)

1,113 – 2,098 M

HIGHER AND FURTHER EDUCATION LECTURERS (group 9–14)

647 – 1,107 M

TECHNICIANS (group 4–9)

It was a quantum leap from the abacus to the pocket calculator. After many centuries of moving beads from one end of a row to the other, mathematicians could obtain answers to complex questions at the touch of a button. The non-programmable floating decimal pocket calculator »SR1« produced by »VEB Mikroelektronik Wilhelm Pieck« in Mühlhausen was designed especially for the needs of school children. Developed by Gerhard Bieber and Hartmut Voigt and released in 1981, some 850,000 such calculators were sold at the subsidized price of 123 Marks. Available only to school children, they needed to present a special coupon in order to qualify for the reduced price. Otherwise they would have to purchase the »MR 609« for 800 Marks. The owner engraved his name on the back of the calculator to prevent theft. Of greater interest was the battery, many of which are still working today.

»LEARN, LEARN AND LEARN AGAIN«

(Vladimir Ilyich Lenin)

Monday morning in the school yard: »Comrade Principal, the school is assembled!« The flag rising slowly, hundreds of school children sang a pioneer song. Education was conceived as the formation of a Socialist citizen and teaching in the social sciences was dominated by the regurgitation of prescribed wisdom. Even the theses of the classic authors of Marxism-Leninism were reduced to a set of stock phrases. University courses repeated exactly the same propositions on a compulsory basic course tested in both written and oral examinations. Those taking a doctoral degree were forced to repeat the material for a third time.

Achievement was very important, and standards were high, especially in mathematics and the natural sciences. Moreover, school did not finish when formal lessons ended for the day; some investigated their surroundings as »young scientists«, whilst others swotted for the Mathematics Olympia. The more sporting opted to train in the gym for a zero-gravity life as a cosmonaut.

Indeed, sport and military training was accorded a prominent place in young people's lives. Sports lessons functioned as pre-military training in another guise and the Society for Sport and Technology (GST) instructed its charges in shooting. Some even took their driving test with the GST. Even university students were subject to weekly (obligatory) sports courses with an examination culminating in a dive from the five-metre board. Every male student was forced to complete a month-long military camp; their female counterparts had to complete a course in civil defence.

A short exercise programme designed to enable school children to sit still, Berlin 1985

The East German education system produced successful athletes, good soldiers, industrious engineers and well-qualified scientists. Yet for all its academic-mindedness, the system frowned on critical thinking. In 1988, four Berlin schoolchildren were expelled for writing a critical article for the school newspaper questioning the sense of the annual military parades. This case caused an uproar; attracting widespread publicity from civil rights activists and the western media, it was only one of many such disciplinary actions, which had hitherto gone unnoticed.

STARTING EARLY

Childcare provision in the DDR was exemplary. Seeking to exploit the employment potential of women, the state provided a sufficient number of crèche and kindergarten places to enable mothers to work. This also enabled the state to begin early with the work of raising its children to become model Socialist citizens. Learning to count using toy tanks and soldiers was common. Seeking to bring children out of their nappies as early as possible, nursery teachers left their charges together on the long potty bench until they were all finished – no-one could get up until the last had »gone«. Writing in the 1990s, the West German criminologist Christian Pfeiffer identified such practices as a possible source of right-wing extremism in East Germany. This so-called »potty debate« soon blew over, and potty banks are still to be found in a number of crèches across eastern Germany, albeit without the ideological undertones.

THE SCHOOL SYSTEM IN THE DDR

- Polytechnic school (POS):
  Schools for ages 4 – 14, attendance was obligatory
- Extended secondary school (EOS): for ages 16–18 resulting in 'A' levels
- School of vocational training: up to three-year college and practice-based training following the POS
- Vocational schools (medical-educational): three-year courses following the POS for careers such as medical assistant or nursery teacher
- Technical college (technical-economic): three-year courses providing vocational training for engineering jobs (without degree)
- University: five-year course of study

THE FURTHER CAREER OF 16 YEAR OLDS IN 1989

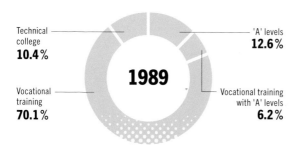

Technical
college
10.4%

'A' levels
12.6%

Vocational
training
70.1%

Vocational training
with 'A' levels
6.2%

1989

LEVELS OF POPULAR QUALIFICATION (FROM 16), 1989

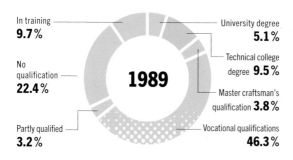

In training
9.7%

University degree
5.1%

Technical college
degree **9.5**%

No
qualification
22.4%

Master craftsman's
qualification **3.8**%

Partly qualified
3.2%

Vocational qualifications
46.3%

1989

NUMBER OF CRÈCHE PLACES PER 1,000 CHILDREN

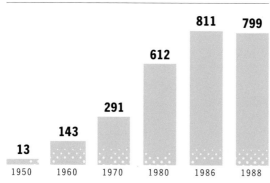

1950	1960	1970	1980	1986	1988
13	**143**	**291**	**612**	**811**	**799**

PLAYING, LEARNING AND WORKING

1

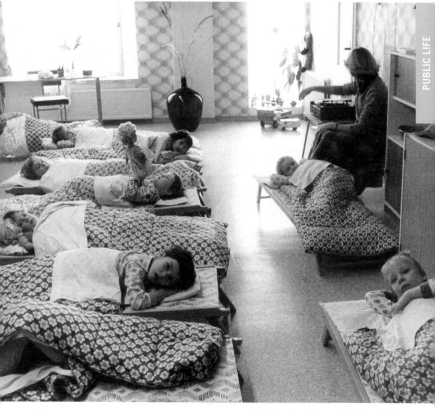

2

1 Kindergarten children celebrating carnival,
Berlin 1980
2 Children taking a nap at a kindergarten,
Schulzendorf 1982

In 1989, 94 per cent of all children were allocated a free place in a state kindergarten. Provision of comprehensive universal childcare from birth enabled the state to mobilize female labour for the short-handed economy; it also enabled the SED to begin early with its programme of indoctrination.

The Ministry of Education established central control over childcare in DDR, instructing their staff to inculcate collectivist values. East German children were to be formed into Socialist personalities from a young age, eschewing infantile individualism for the maturity of collective group awareness.

A strict daily routine placed a strong emphasis on hygiene and healthy living and the Socialist virtues of obedience, discipline, orderliness and hard work. Children were to be turned into Socialists by playing collectively, reading and writing about Socialism and visiting nationalized industries and the Army. They were also expected to perform minor tasks such as setting the meal table and clearing away their toys. Circumventing these directives, the kindergarten teachers often just employed common sense and friendliness to ensure that children grew up in a loving and nurturing environment.

PROPORTION OF CHILDREN WITH A KINDERGARTEN PLACE

34.5 % 46.1 % 46.5 % 92.2 % 90.5 % 94.0 %

1955   1960   1970   1980   1984   1988

53

OLYMPICS ALL THE YEAR ROUND

Sport was very important in the DDR and was made available to all. The right to sport was enshrined in the constitution, which made sure that Walter Ulbricht's dictum — »every man, everywhere — sport once a week!« — could be realized. Private sporting associations were closed and all sporting activity was arranged under the German Gymnastics and Sporting League (Deutscher Turn- und Sportbund, DTSB) which maintained a range of Company Sport Associations (Betriebssportgemeinschaften, BSG) financed by the employer.

Workers could choose from a range of sporting activities and join any club free-of-charge. They could even apply for leave from work to take part in organized sporting events or assist in their planning and realization. Such competitions were organized for every age group to encourage the nation into communal fitness. For its part, the press never tired of extolling the virtues of good honest competitive sweat.

Although East Germans were not required to pay for sport, an insufficient number of sports halls and swimming pools and the poor quality of the equipment meant that not everybody was able to play as much as they would have liked. Talent spotters were always on the look-out for gifted children, who were whisked off to well-equipped sports schools at a very young age, and trained to be the world-champions of tomorrow. The state placed great store by med-als — especially Olympic medals — and spared no cost to ensure that they produced winners in every generation.

The overperformance of the DDR in international sport for a nation of its size was not just the product of hard work, but due to the widespread use of doping. Doctors and trainers administered vast quantities of »Oral-Turinabol« to their charges, including young children, and often without their knowledge. The authorities knew just what they were doing, and were not surprised by the side-effects, illnesses and even deaths in which this policy resulted. They were far more concerned with the prestige and victory of Socialism.

1 Walter Ulbricht visits the III. Deutsche Turn- und Sportfest in Leipzig, 1959
2 (next page) Participants at the FDJ Whitsun meeting at the Stadion der Weltjugend, 1989

1

SPORT HURTS

Copious amounts of Oral-Turinabol were administered to professional sportsmen and women from the 1970s. The anabolic steroid strengthens muscles and raises levels of aggression and risk-taking. Trainers even gave the drugs to children, passing them off as »vitamins«. Such »treatment« brings the risk of dangerous side-effects for the liver and hormone balance. Many athletes suffered considerable lasting damage. Others died.

YEAR	LOCATION	GOLD	SILVER	BRONZE	RANK

MEDALS AT THE SUMMER GAMES

YEAR	LOCATION	GOLD	SILVER	BRONZE	RANK
1968	Mexico	9	9	7	5
1972	Munich	20	3	23	3
1976	Montreal	40	25	25	2
1980	Moscow	47	37	42	2
1984	LA »boycotted by the DDR«				
1988	Seoul	37	35	30	2

MEDALS AT THE WINTER GAMES

YEAR	LOCATION	GOLD	SILVER	BRONZE	RANK
1968	Grenoble	1	2	2	10
1972	Sapporo	4	3	7	2
1976	Innsbruck	7	5	7	2
1980	Lake Placid	9	7	7	2
1984	Sarajevo	9	9	6	1
1988	Calgary	9	10	6	2

ADVENTURE HOLIDAYS ON A LOW BUDGET

Many East Germans dreamt of holidaying on a Mediterranean beach, but in vain. Even those businessmen, artists and scientists permitted to travel to western countries for professional reasons were not allowed to take their family on holiday in the »Non-Socialist Currency Area«. A typical summer holiday began in February with an application to the travel department of the »Free German Trade Union Federation« (FDGB), the largest provider of holidays in the DDR. Unbeatably good value, the packages they provided even included heavily reduced train tickets to get there. Nevertheless, the dream tickets to the Baltic Sea were so scarce that would-be holiday-makers needed good contacts or considerable luck to obtain them. The same applied to holiday accommodation in Thuringia and to winter holidays in the Harz Mountains. Even those managing to get away were faced with a modest standard of comfort: communal bathrooms and canteen meals were standard. Company-owned holiday homes often provided a greater level of comfort, but at the cost of going on holiday

with one's colleagues. Those unwilling to put up with all these drawbacks simply bought a tent and went camping. They still had to book however.

Relaxed border controls after 1972 meant that the penniless young could hitch-hike to Warsaw or Prague, cities which provided a little more freedom and glamour. Here, they could read western newspapers and watch films banned back home. There were even more records on sale. The growth of the Polish civil rights movement meant that this haven of freedom was closed to East German citizens from 30 October 1980. It was feared that East Germans might come back with the wrong ideas. Other holiday-makers travelled even further, investigating the Black Sea Coast, Lake Balaton or the High Tatras — adventures which were difficult to book and very expensive. Once arrived, holiday-makers experienced numerous hurdles to achieving any level of comfort — the DDR Mark was not an attractive currency and hoteliers responded by extending preferential treatment to the holders of somewhat harder currencies.

The Möller family from
Staßfurt camping in
Prerow (Baltic Sea), 1988

POLITICS WITHOUT SWIMMING TRUNKS

At the beach, East Germans preferred nudism. The success of
the »FKK« movement was less the result of a desire for greater
sexual freedom than a desire to do something forbidden. Just
once. Moreover, many Communists saw nudity as an expression
of true classlessness. Whatever the reason, it was not due to a
shortage of swimwear.

CUBA
1,283

HOLIDAY DESTINATIONS ISSUED
TO DDR CITIZENS, 1988

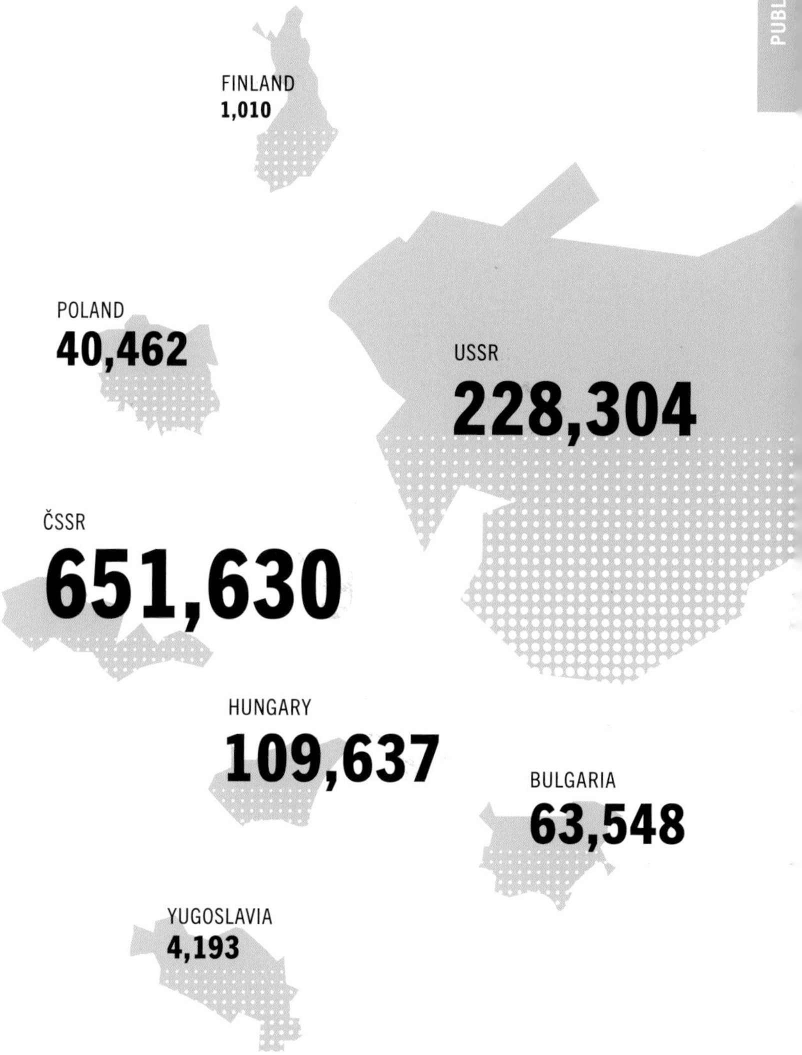

FINLAND
1,010

POLAND
40,462

USSR
228,304

ČSSR
651,630

HUNGARY
109,637

BULGARIA
63,548

YUGOSLAVIA
4,193

PARTY AND STATE

BUST OF LENIN
THE MAN OF GRANITE

The large crowd of East Berliners gathered on Leninplatz on 19 April 1970 – the newspapers reported up to 200,000 people – watched the unveiling of the monument to Vladimir Ilyich Lenin. Dominating the sterile vista of tower block flats in Friedrichshain, the red granite likeness of the Russian revolutionary informed the world that had he lived, he would now be 100 years old. 1970 was proclaimed the »Year of Lenin« and his face was now ubiquitous – glaring from every newspaper, displayed on television programmes and portrayed in a range of feature films. There were even jokes about Lenin. Some were better than others, all are untranslatable. Perhaps it was only the jokes that really made Lenin come alive. The plethora of busts and images which littered the republic proclaimed not a man of flesh and blood, but a myth which had been embroidered over the last fifty years. Nobody read his books for fun or even for interest – they had become purely instruments of propaganda.

Many still see Lenin as the representative of an ideal which was later betrayed. After all, did he not fight with his dying breath to prevent Stalin from assuming control of the Soviet Union? Whatever the truth, he fashioned the structures and practices of Communist rule which were used to murder millions of people. This explains the move after 1989 to take down his statues, one of which can now be viewed in an exhibition in Spandau. Perhaps the statues have found a purpose after all – to act as a warning from history.

PARTY AND STATE

1

»The comrades are still in the meeting« was a common phrase often heard in offices and companies. Levels of Party membership increased as you moved up the social scale. Whilst manual workers were underrepresented, a large proportion of academics and teachers could call themselves »comrade«; almost all managers had a Party card. Those summoned at irregular intervals to a Party meeting could imagine themselves close to the heart of power, but in reality, they had little influence on affairs. Never-

theless, a comrade found out early what was going on, and was on first name terms with all the important people in his company.

Those wanting to make a career in East Germany had to join the SED. The membership fee was negligible, but the real price of membership was high. The Party demanded not only absolute loyalty and iron discipline, but complete openness, even about personal matters. Required to attend meetings and training days, the comrades were also drafted in

2

1 XI SED Party Conference in the Palace of
the Republic, 1986
2 Walter Ulbricht receives his birthday guests
wearing his slippers and dressing gown, 1971

to manage the Mass Organizations, run the elections and even join the paramilitary formations attached to every company. An appeal to the Party members could never be refused. Transgressions were met with a catalogue of punishments culminating in expulsion from the Party. This produced an indelible black mark in the cadre file, which brought a lifetime of consequences.

The constitution of the DDR accorded the SED a »leading role« in the running of the country, but there were no laws defining what this actually meant in real terms. In practice, however, wherever a Party member was to be found, he was the one making all the important decisions. This principle was inviolate: the »comrade« in the bakery was in charge; the General Secretary of the SED was usually the head of state. Walter Ulbricht occupied the office from

TIMELINE

1945

The ban on the Communist Party of Germany (KPD) and the Social Democratic Party of Germany (SPD) is lifted in the Soviet zone of occupation

1948

The transformation of the SED into a Stalinist cadre party

1953

The death of Stalin and announcement of the New Course. The People's Uprising on 17 June

1946

The forced union of the KPD and SPD to form the Socialist Unity Party of Germany (SED)

1960–1971 and, although he remained nominally the head of state until 1973, he was removed from his Party office in 1971 and suffered a humiliating loss of power. His subservience was completed later that year, when he was photographed receiving his birthday guests in his slippers and dressing gown. The Party wanted to show him who was in charge. The new strong man was Erich Honecker, General Secretary of the Party after 1971 and after 1976 also head of state.

The Politburo functioned as a sort of all-powerful shadow government with authority over all areas of Party and State. The system of government in the DDR abandoned all modern developments in state practice such as the separation of powers or the redress of grievance. As such, East Germany did not separate the functions of the legislative, executive and judiciary, but concentrated all power in the hands of the SED. The ministries and other offices of the state were not insignificant, but always acted to implement the will of the Party.

Economic policy was also the preserve of the Party and was implemented through the centralization of ownership. In this context, »People's ownership« meant state ownership. State planning commissions drafted an annual national plan and passed

1956

XX. Party Conference of
the Soviet Communist
party begins de-Stalinization

1971

The transfer of power from Walter Ulbricht to
Erich Honecker. The VIII. Party Conference
announces the Unity of Economic and Social Policy

1990

1963

VI. Party Conference.
Announcement of the New
Economic System of Planning
and Management of Economy

1985

Gorbachev begins
his reforms in the
Soviet Union

1989

The SED loses power
and renames itself as
the Party of Democratic
Socialism (PDS)

laws stipulating what each company was to produce. The same principles applied to education, research, culture and all other aspects of life, which were ruled over by the Party. This was all very convenient for a Party concerned to maintain its iron grip on power, but it made change almost impossible. Ruling that there would be no debates or even questions, the SED expected absolute obedience. When the Party collapsed in 1989, it pulled down the entire edifice of power with it.

Photograph DDR Museum

TWO PLUS TWO
MAKES FIVE

Perhaps the last unknown about the DDR is the question of sincerity: did its rulers and their henchmen actually believe what they parroted or was it just a means to an end? Almost in despair, the singer Wolf Biermann asked the Party functionaries in a song: »what do you have between your ears — filth or straw? Are you really stupid, or are you just pretending?« One thing was certain: the ideology was not just there for show. The all-pervading Marxism-Leninism was the only legitimate world view in the DDR. Repeated ad nauseam, most schoolchildren could recite its central tenets in their sleep. The destination of history is Communism; the road to this happy goal leads through Socialism in the form existing in the DDR. western Capitalism was currently in its death throes, and the Working Class — led by the Communist Party — was about to overthrow it. Learnt in school, this wisdom sufficed even for doctoral examinations. Although the escapist nature of these beliefs made it difficult to take them seriously, this did not prevent many from so doing.

The DDR did hold room for a great deal of hypocrisy and deviousness and even a measure of schizophrenia, but the majority of functionaries were not mere cynics. Were the Party to announce that two plus two made five, they would believe it, ascribing it to

Televised transmission of the V Turn-
und Sportfest der DDR in Leipzig, 1969

the »higher truths« on which the Party based its pronouncements. »Marxism is omnipotent because it is true« as Lenin taught. Such circular argumentation is irrefutable. Those not prepared to accept the ideological superiority of Marxism soon experienced its wrath. There were many channels for this anger — ranging from exclusion from education and professional training to imprisonment — all of which were very persuasive. SED agitators did not see the point of discussions with the mistaken. Wolf Biermann gave a clear answer to his question in his ballad to the »Truly Concerned Friend«: »They are that stupid, but they are also pretending.«

The ceremonial unveiling of the Karl Marx monument in Karl-Marx-Stadt (today Chemnitz); FDJ and pioneers declare their loyalty to Marxism-Leninism, 1971

Bearing a closer resemblance to Gutenberg's printing press from 1450 than modern technology, the printing press in our exhibition was the key weapon in the arsenal of the East German opposition. In the 1970s, several small and independent groups began to use the safety of the Church to print underground journals. Writing about the environment, freedom and human rights, they were able to circumvent tight legislation by marking their publications »for internal church use only«. Their papers on the environment, called »Umweltblätter«, published in a small print run of 200, were an important part of their output. The »Umwelt-bibliothek«, an environmental pressure group, printed them on the press displayed here, which used to be located in the basement of the »Zions-kirche« in Berlin's Prenzlauer Berg.

Despite its small size and impact, the state reacted hysterically. A raid on the premises of the »Umweltbib-liothek« on 24 November 1987, did not solve the problem for the Stasi,

as protestors staged a candle-light vigil in front of the church demanding the release of those arrested. With similar protests springing up all over

East Germany and covered by the West German media, the SED feared that the situation would escalate. Backing down, they released the prisoners and even returned the printing press. Even though the SED controlled a massive propaganda apparatus, it had been brought down by 200 small, poorly-printed pamphlets. David had beaten Goliath again.

A MIGHTY FORTRESS IS OUR GOD

The SED did everything they could to force the Church to the margins of society. Nevertheless, the Church buildings retained their impressive presence in the urban landscape, and with their doors wide open every Sunday, everyone could enter. With Church attendance on the decline, visitors to a church entered what was to them an entirely foreign world. They came for many reasons. Some wanted to look at the works of art, whilst many listened to the organ music. Others sought peace and quiet away from the uproar of everyday life. Even more were searching for answers to forbidden questions. Even if sometimes unintentional, the Lutheran Church represented the greatest of challenges to the state. A visible challenge to the Party's monopoly on truth, its rule ended at the church door. Having had some bad experiences with the Church, the state became wise enough to avoid direct confrontation. Its attempts in 1953 to repress the »Young Church« ended in a fiasco and in the aftermath of the uprising of 17 June, the state was forced to revise its policy of expelling Christians from further and higher education. This policy was replaced by general discrimi-

The demolition of the »Versöhnungskirche« in the death strip, 28.01.1985

nation against Christians in schools, training and the professions. The long-term success of this new policy was matched only by its perfidious nature. The death of Pastor Oskar Brüsewitz — after setting himself on fire on Zeitz market place in 1976 in protest against the persecution of the Church — shifted attention to the situation of young Christians. Unable to contain its unease any longer, the Church opened its doors to those seeking alternatives and they gathered in the Church-based environmental and peace groups and within its social work. Unhappy with the new develop-

ments, many in the Church hierarchy tried to restrain its more impulsive brethren — often with a Biblical »justification«.

Undeterred, a number of pastors and church councils protected these new groups, granting access to rooms, telephones and duplicating machines. Providing the framework for a nascent public sphere, it is impossible to over-estimate the importance of the Churches in the turbulent events of late 1989. Starting with a number of small candle-bearing groups gathering in front of the Republic's many churches, the autumn revolution came from within the Lutheran Church.

RELIGIOUS AFFILIATION IN THE DDR

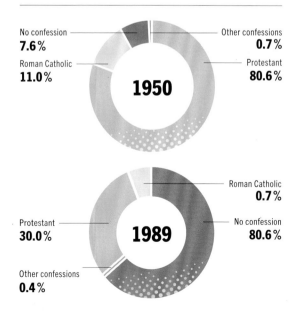

No confession
7.6%

Roman Catholic
11.0%

Other confessions
0.7%

Protestant
80.6%

1950

Roman Catholic
0.7%

Protestant
30.0%

No confession
80.6%

Other confessions
0.4%

1989

WALKING TALL

East German citizens learnt the value of silence and evasion from an early age. If the teacher wanted to find out who amongst her class watched West German television, she would ask innocently how the Sandman (a popular children's television programme, rival versions of which were broadcast in the East and West) arrived yesterday. The worldly-wise children would smile knowingly and reply »on a moon rocket with a large red star on its nose«. Even if they had watched the West German version, they knew better than to let on. The guiding principle of East German life, whether for young or old was »ignorance is bliss my friend«. People were less afraid of a run-in with the Stasi, and more governed by a general desire to keep one's head down and go through life without attracting too much attention. Once earned, a black mark in your record remained there for the rest of your life.

Many people found such an existence unbearable and learnt to vent their spleen in private, whilst toeing the Party line at work. Others, tired of never-ending hypocrisy, accepted the negative consequences of honesty; whilst yet more decided to make small compromises so as to exercise a positive influence in their immediate surroundings. Whatever the merits of these various positions, it did not amount to political opposition. Indeed, what could you really do? Small individual actions such as handing out protest leaflets or daubing slogans on a wall achieved little, yet could be met with serious punishment.

The leeway for action began to increase in the 1980s. Official DDR support for the peace movement in West Germany meant that it could hardly punish those of its citizens who called for the removal of Soviet warheads from the DDR, whilst the government itself was demanding that the US withdraw its nuclear arsenal from West Germany. Moreover, the protection provided by the Lutheran Church for the East German peace movement conferred it with a certain freedom of action. Choosing as their symbol the Old Testament motif of »swords into ploughshares« designed by a Soviet artist, they claimed not to be an opposition movement, whilst acting as such. Playing to a very small (but highly effective) audience, they had to tread carefully when opposing a ruthless and highly organized state.

Prayers for peace in the Nikolaikirche (Leipzig) out of which the Monday Demonstrations developed, 1989

CHRONOLOGY

1950

School children protest against the undemocratic elections to the East German Parliament

1956

Students and intellectuals protest against Stalinism

1968

Youth protests against the suppression of the Prague Spring

1953

16/17 June – strikes and demonstrations develop into a national uprising

1976

The writers' protest against the expulsion of Wolf Biermann

1988

The arrest of protesters at the official Luxemburg-Liebknecht demonstrations sparks a protest movement

1979

Formation of the independent peace movement »Swords into Ploughshares«

1987

Vigils in the Zionkirche (Berlin) in protest against the arrest of activists from the »Umweltbibliothek«

1989

Protests against electoral fraud

Protest against the Tiananmen square massacre

Appeal from the New Forum to constitute an opposition movement outside the Lutheran Church

Foundation of the Social Democratic Party in the DDR

7-9 October, demonstrations in Leipzig, Berlin and elsewhere initiate the Peaceful Revolution

GOING FOLDING

The whole rotten business uncovered on 7 May 1989 meant that long-held suspicions finally became a certainty. The fantastic results (up to 99 per cent) achieved by the state after every election were the result of manipulation. Where pressure, propaganda and the lack of alternatives failed, the SED leadership simply cheated and published incorrect figures.

Judging by appearances, polling day on 7 May was like any other. State propaganda pulled out all the stops. Wearing their Sunday best, happy people carried placards bearing »DDR – My Fatherland« and billboards exhorted passers-by to support the National Front. Polling stations were flanked by students in FDJ blue and flag-waving children. Those staying at home received a visit from officials, reminding them of their civic duty. Amidst this close observance of the old rituals, there were small differences. The proportion of people using the polling booths was considerably higher than previous years, when the folded ballot paper

1

was cast in the ballot box directly after its issue. Going to the booth was a dangerous and brave act. Despite official claims to the contrary, elections were not free, the ballot was not secret and the systems were not transparent.

The act of voting was popularly referred to as »going folding«, as little more was required. The lists of the National Front were filled with the nominations of the SED. There were no boxes on the ballot slip to make any crosses and rejection was not really part of the plan. A »no« vote required the citizen to cross through every single name on the list. All those taking the brave step of using the polling booth (located in the furthest corner of the room) had first to pass the massed ranks of election officials, who would suspect them of being a subversive enemy. Shortly before the closure of

the polling stations on the evening of 7 May, a number of people suddenly arrived to observe the proceedings. Checking the count, they registered up to 20 per cent »no« votes in some polling stations. This was not reflected in the official return of 98.85 per cent of »yes« votes. Going public with their findings, civil rights activists organized protests on the Alexanderplatz on every 7th day of the following months. The protest of 7 October 1989 sparked a course of events which culminated in the Peaceful Revolution.

1 Heinz Quermann casts his vote at local elections in 1989, the last election conducted in accordance with DDR rules, Köpenick (Berlin) 7.5.1989

PLAYING AT PARLIAMENT

No one provided a better summary of Communist policy in May 1945 than Walter Ulbricht. Faced by considerable impatience from his comrades at the need to share power with bourgeois and Christian Democratic parties he replied: »it has to look democratic but we've got to have everything under our control.« In addition on to the working-class parties of the KPD (Communist Party of Germany) and SPD (Social Democratic Party of Germany), the middleclass CDU (Christian Democratic Union of Germany) and Liberal Democratic Party of Germany (LDP, later renamed the LDPD) were also licensed as political parties. Initially they were given considerable room for manoeuvre, but the freedoms of the bourgeois parties were curtailed in 1947/8. The CDU, LDP and the subsequently founded National Democratic Party of Germany (NDPD) and the Democratic Peasants Party of Germany (DBD) along with the mass organizations

NDPD
140,000
MEMBERS

EXORIENTE PAX
CDU
140,000
MEMBERS

DEMOKRATISCHE BAUERNPARTEI DEUTSCHLANDS
DBD
117,000
MEMBERS

were subsumed under the organizational straitjacket of the National Front. The parties of the democratic bloc – hence their name the »bloc parties« – were now firmly integrated into the SED system of rule. These organizations catered for all tastes – former Nazis and officers found a welcome in the NDPD; artisans and businessmen were integrated into the LDPD and independent farmers joined the DBD.

Christianity was difficult to integrate. Despite the irreconcilable claims of Christianity and Marxism-Leninism, the SED wanted Christians to work with them in the establishment of the DDR. The bloc parties were all given equal representation in the East German Parliament, the State Council and the district and municipal assemblies, but received nowhere near the number of seats allocated to the SED. Raising their hands dutifully to every proposal made by the SED, the parties even voted against the interests of their own members and in 1972, the LDPD gave its approval to the expropriation of the remnants of private industry. CDU representatives were given functions in the cultural sphere, their cooperation appeared to indicate the reconciliation of Marxism and Christianity. Nobody dwelt on the fact that Christian children were systematically denied access to further and higher education.

Those wanting to make a career often saw membership of one of the bloc parties as a necessary compromise with the system. Really senior positions were however only filled by SED members. As a result, the bloc parties were often despised by both sides – by the general public for their opportunism and obsequiousness and by the SED for their potential unreliability. For their part, the members of these parties felt they had the opportunity to effect positive change within their immediate environments. Nevertheless, the price for this choice was a public and unambiguous commitment to the DDR and Socialism.

106,000 MEMBERS

Number of members of the bloc parties, 28.2.1990

85

FROM THE »I«
TO THE »WE«

4

2

3

1

The collective was more important than the individual; SED functionaries never tired of celebrating the victory of the »we« over the »I«. Focussing on attracting as many people as possible to »mass organizations« of workers, women and children, the state sought to exercise control in groups. Presiding over all these conglomerations was the Party. According to the SED propaganda, the life of the class enemy in the West was characterized by egoism, loneliness and social indifference. Comrades in the DDR on the other hand, enjoyed the solidarity, public spirit and social warmth of Socialism. How willing a person was to accept and enjoy the advantages provided by the Socialist community became clear in school. The first indication was membership of the Pioneers and the Free German Youth (FDJ), a loyalty test which the majority passed with flying colours. There were always two or three in the class who refused, but it was clear that they ran the risk of discrimination in later life. The rest of the class took part, most out of a sense of duty and with marginal interest, some with real enthusiasm. The FDJ provided them with camping trips, choirs and poetry seminars. As the only officially permitted youth organization, it was charged with the task of forming the youth into »class-conscious Socialists«, a task in which it experienced

6

8

5

7

9

only moderate success. The mass organizations gave the DDR a vaguely democratic appearance. All FDJ members were eligible to stand and vote in elections for the more minor offices. Many did so and some became treasurers, secretaries or group leaders. Holding such offices in the FDJ, otherwise known as the »fighting reserve of the Party« was good for your future career prospects.

Having left the FDJ, adults did not lack opportunities to collect membership books, badges and emblems. Those not wishing to join the SED or one of the bloc parties could enter the Free German Trade Union Federation (FDGB), or the Democratic Women's League of Germany (DFD), leap around in the German Gymnastics and Sporting Association (DTSB), or join the Allotment and Small Animal Bree-

ding Association (VKSK) or the Society for German–Soviet Friendship (DSF). Nevertheless, the »social activity« of the majority of group members was limited to payment of the membership fee. Above all, a person's membership of mass organizations served to mitigate the suspicion of the authorities.

---

1 Kulturbund / 2 Freie Deutsche Jugend / 3 Deutscher Turn- und Sportbund der DDR / 4 Gesellschaft für Sport und Technik / 5 Freier Deutscher Gewerkschaftsbund / 6 Verband der Kleingärtner, Siedler und Kleintierzüchter / 7 Vereinigung der gegenseitigen Bauernhilfe / 8 Demokratischer Frauenbund Deutschlands / 9 Deutsch-Sowjetische Freundschaft

In 1977, the Central Committee of the SED was told: »The gap between us and the competition in microelectronics amounts to up to 9 years«. The SED was alarmed, as it had invested much hope in the home-grown elec-

1 MBIT CHIP
HONECKER'S PATH TO GLORY

tronics industry. It was supposed to modernize the export industries – especially through the use of CAD/CAM technology in the mechanical engineering industry – and save the ailing East German economy. Unable to purchase western technology (the Capitalists decided not to assist the Eastern bloc by selling such impor-

tant goods), the SED concentrated on closing the gap through industrial espionage and spending billions on research. The 1 Mbit chip was presented to Erich Honecker in 1988. Able to store around 35 lines of type-written script, it still lagged far behind its western counterparts – Toshiba had recently rolled out a 4 Mbit chip – and was horrendously expensive. In the end, only a few hundred of these chips were produced. In the electronics branch, as in many other sectors, the DDR was never going to catch up.

A PLANNED ECONOMY WITHOUT A PLAN

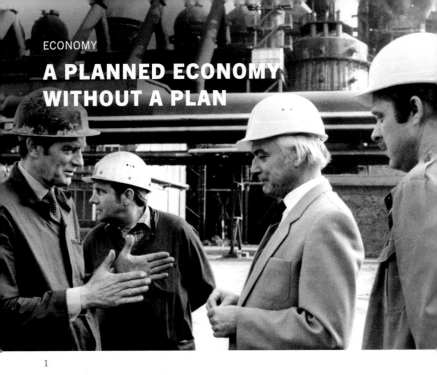

1

The work of DDR economists resembled that of medieval alchemists, labouring for a tyrannical overlord in an attempt to turn base metals into gold. Some even began to suspect that their labour was in vain, based, as it had to be, on false premises. Just as the feudal lords had proven resistant to all evidence, the SED blocked their ears to any protests and merely ordered their minions to redouble their efforts. In the early 1950s, the state sought to emulate the Soviet model, concentrating on developing heavy industry. Steel works were built from scratch and whole towns emerged around them. One example was Stalinstadt, later renamed Eisenhüttenstadt. However, such projects remained uncompetitive.

The priority accorded to heavy industry in the 1950s (powered by brown coal) was abandoned in 1959. The magic formula was now »chemistry brings bread, prosperity and beauty«. Industry was reoriented towards chemicals and the refinement of Soviet oil sourced at reduced prices. This was accompanied by reform of the structures of the economy. Less planning, greater individual responsibility and a dose of market forces were all designed to bring better products and higher productivity. Performance-related pay was another innovation. The whole system was designated »The System of Material Leverage«. The New Economic System of Planning contained a number of good ideas, but nevertheless failed to address the problem of fixed retail prices and the rigidity of economic planning. The 1960s also saw the advent of another »panacea«, this time in the form of Science and Technology. Cybernetics was to bring the solution to all problems. As one contemporary joke ran »In 1965, the

1 Director of Research Dr. Manfred Drodowsky talking to metal workers in »Bandstahlkombinat Hermann Matern«, Eisenhüttenstadt 1984
2 The »Industrieverband Fahrzeugbau (IFA)« stand at the Leipzig Autumn fair, 1975

SED fed in East German economic data to a Russian computer. After much whirring of cogs, the instructions were printed: Depose the Politburo of the SED!« The problem was that the computer lacked a class standpoint. It followed the dictates of logic, not the Party line.

With the »Unity of Social and Economic Policy« launched in the 1970s, expensive social provision diverted funds away from necessary economic and industrial investment. This crisis was compounded by the increase in commodity prices and most importantly, the price of Soviet oil. Falling into a chronic debt-spiral, in 1983, the DDR was forced to beg for a massive loan from West Germany. Access to foreign currency was possible only through producing competitive exports. Grasping at straws, the SED leadership found a new panacea: the production of a

1 Mbit memory chip was intended to enable the East German engineering sector to implement an export boom which would resuscitate Socialism. As the new leaders installed in October 1989 began to audit the East German accounts, their economists were now free to tell the hard truth: the DDR could only be saved at the price of cuts in social spending by up to a third, involving competitive rents, increased prices and reduced benefits. Aware that angry East Germans would never accept such a step, the SED chose to shut up shop. Socialism ended in much the same manner as a company which knew it was bankrupt but sought to paper over the cracks. Those responsible fled the scene and left the problem to the liquidators.

91

1

1 The Chemical works Bitterfeld, one of the largest pesticides works in the DDR with c. 20,000 employees, 1981
2 The selection of Bighead carp for spawning at »VEB Binnenfischerei Peitz«, the largest carp producer in the DDR, 1988
3 Series production of the automatic SLR miniature camera »Practica EE2« in »VEB Pentacon Dresden«, 1978

2

1 Staking out the land reform, autumn 1945
2 Tractors arrive at the APG Batzlow
(Strausberg) c. 1960

1

between demand and supply, the state decided on the full collectivization of agriculture. The programme of forming Agricultural Production Collectives (»Landwirtschaftliche Produktionsgenossenschaften«, LPG), was unrolled slowly and completed in 1960. Although the farmers theoretically retained control over their livestock and produce, in practice they worked as employees of vast state-owned farms. Only in this way was the state able to produce enough food to satisfy both domestic demand and the need to export internationally. Privatized after 1990, the LPGs were one of the few East German industries to prosper in the Capitalist world.

2

Despite propagating the classless society, East German politicians made sure that they enjoyed a number of privileges, including comfortable transport. Not satisfied with a Trabant or Wartburg, they decided to buy in Sweden and came back with a gleaming fleet of Volvos. Convinced not just by their fuel-economy and reliability, DDR policy makers decided that only a touch of Scandinavian glamour would convince the world that East Germany was a modern and cosmopolitan country. Erich Honecker himself was chauffeured in a Citroën.

The Volvo 264 TE (Top Executive) in our exhibition has a V6 motor and dates from 1982. The large rear section has the usual seating plus two extra seats facing backwards to enable meetings. In addition to comfort, the passengers also enjoyed privacy, thanks to a set of curtains.

THE VOLVO

- Date of construction: 1982
- Only 335 sold between 1976 and 1984
- Motor: V6, 2,664 cm^3, type B28E
- Power: 156 hp
- Top speed: c. 170 km/h
- Length: 5.60 m

GOLDEN CHAINS

Erich Honecker's former house, Wandlitz, 2017

»Fat cats« muttered the people on the pavement as the large fleet of Volvos rushed past carrying the leaders of Party and State. With the entire traffic halted to allow the escorted motorcade to pass, the average East German had plenty to complain about. »So, a Soviet ›Tschaika‹ is not good enough for our comrades — they need a limousine from Sweden. And we have to wait centuries for a naff car made of cardboard«. Complaints also abounded about the practice of painting the buildings flanking the regular routes travelled by these motorcades — but only as high as the passengers in the back seats could see. The houses on the back streets remained a uniform grey. Did the members of the Politburo actually believe what they saw? After all, they could have found out the reality from the Stasi reports which regularly landed on their desks. Perhaps they read these reports whilst relaxing deep into the comfortable upholstery of their ministerial cars, racing across a land with which they had lost touch? None of them ever thought to enter a shop in one of the side streets, to order a beer in one of the run-down pubs. This might have boosted their popularity. Secluded from real life by their bodyguards and surrounded by servile subordinates, the oppressors of fellow citizens were themselves prisoners of their own system.

Housed in a woodland settlement in Wandlitz just North of Berlin, the standard of living enjoyed by the ruling circle did not match the luxury of western heads of state. Indeed, they lived a highly unsophisticated life in modest 1950s houses. Very few made use of the swimming pool or the moderately-priced restaurant made available to them — probably afraid of meeting an enemy from the Politburo. Their wives on the other hand, enjoyed going shopping in the shops selling a number of West German products — a dream for the average DDR citizen. Many of the functionaries spent their weekends in hunting lodges, attempting to murder a few well-fed roebucks. Stasi boss Mielke had a number of antlers in his lodge. What is left of all of this? Perhaps only a verse from Wolf Biermann:

»I see your gobs every morning in the papers but we will soon forget you!«

»GHETTO OF THE BIGWIGS«, LOCATION PLAN, 1988

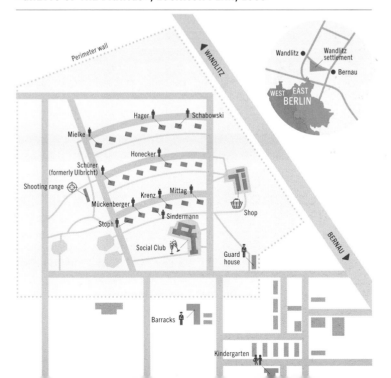

Perimeter wall

WANDLITZ

Wandlitz •   Wandlitz settlement

WEST   EAST   • Bernau
BERLIN

Hager   Schabowski

Mielke

Honecker

Schürer
(formerly Ulbricht)

Shooting range

Krenz   Mittag

Mückenberger

Shop

Stoph

Sindermann

Social Club

Guard house

BERNAU

Barracks

Kindergarten

KALASHNIKOV
THE SOLDIER'S BRIDE

As all East German schoolboys completed some form of pre-military training, they were familiar with many aspects of military service. Nevertheless, nothing prepared the new recruits for some of the new relationships they were expected to enter. It was with no little trepidation that they were introduced to what the instructors referred to as the »soldier's bride« – the AK 47 fully-automatic self-loading rifle, popularly known as the Kalashnikov. Probably having hoped to spend his time with something a little more comely, the recruit made his peace with his new acquaintance and set about learning to hit the target. Cleaning and re-assembling his bride was a key part of basic training. Going out was a little more difficult, however: wanting to keep her beautiful, the soldier went on manoeuvres with a wooden copy.

Developed by Michail Kalaschnikov in 1947 as the »Avtomat Kalaschnikova« (»Kalashnikov's Automatic Gun«), the origin of the popular name is easy to discern. Simple to operate and virtually immune to dirt, damp or mishandling, the AK 47 is a first-class weapon for inexperienced troops. This explains why nearly every conflict in the world features the »Kalashnikov«.

The »Kalashnikov« in our exhibition has been disabled, yet still looks threatening.

»SOVIET SOLDIERS, WE THANK YOU!«

Popping the champagne corks on 7 November 1967, all the important people gathered in the Soviet embassy on East Berlin's Unter den Linden to celebrate the fiftieth anniversary of the »Great Socialist October Revolution«. The marathon of celebrations involving military displays, pathos-laden speeches, monumental concerts and dance festivals was rounded-off with a spectacular celebratory banquet. This orgy of spectacle matched the size of the claim – the founding myth of a world empire. The Socialist brother states from Cuba to North Korea all sent telegrams, gifts and delegations to Moscow to congratulate their big brother.

Not wanting to be outdone, the DDR organized a series of lectures, films and book publications. The bosses of the Academy of Arts and the state record company »VEB Deutsche Schallplatten« even managed to convince the egocentric singer Ernst Busch (better known as the »Red Orpheus«) to produce a German-Soviet song cycle. The resulting record with a John Heartfield cover was presented to a Soviet delegation at a ceremony in Berlin, an event broadcast on live television. The presentation was accompanied by a performance from the sexagenarian Busch, whose rendition of the songs moved his Soviet guests to tears. The more sober response of the East German television audience reflected their true feelings towards the international Socialist brotherhood, amounting as it did, to a forced union.

Even the large membership of the Society for German-Soviet Friendship (DSF) could not hide the latent scepticism towards all things Russian. With a subscription of only a few pfennigs, this Society allowed a number of people to demonstrate the expected »social engagement« at no great cost, whilst leaving maintenance of the much-lauded »steadfast friendship with the Soviet Union« to the Socialist patriarchs such as Ernst Busch. Learning of the Stalinist crimes during his Moscow exile 1935–1937, the actor and singer maintained a steadfast silence about the darker side of Communism throughout his entire life.

Such silence did little however to diminish the poor image of the USSR. Far from a friend, the »Russe« was seen exclusively as an occupier and the compulsory Russian as the first foreign language in schools was never popular. Knowledge of the language was of little value, as few were permitted to travel to Russia and Russian was even more unpopular and less widely spoken in the areas of the Eastern bloc to which ordinary East Germans could travel.

The situation changed only after the rise of Mikhail Gorbachev in 1985. Intrigued by Glasnost and Perestroika, many East Germans frantically tried to brush up their Russian in order to be able to read »Pravda« in the original. Membership of the DSF suddenly assumed a subversive character and readings from Russian authors, Russian film presentations and art exhibitions all began to incur SED suspicion. The German-language magazine »Sputnik«, published by the Soviet Union was never really very popular and attracted a small readership. This changed overnight, and the ban imposed by the SED in October 1988 on its import transformed it into a desirable item. The humourists spoke of a new »Sputnik shock«, reminiscent of the launch of the eponymous satellite in 1957.

THE ARMED PEACE

They tried everything, even getting blind drunk the night before the medical. Yet nothing helped. Balance problems, pale skin, even short-term blindness did not prevent classification as »fully fit for service in the National People's Army«. After the usual diagnosis of flat and splay feet, a bent spine and slight deafness, the recruit was then sent directly to the recruiting board where the decision was made as to the length of service – the minimum of 18 months or a full three years. Some were even »persuaded« to enrol as a professional commissioned officer. A whole range of enticement and threats were employed to extract a »voluntary commitment« to a life in the army. The recruit was faced with a difficult task — that of refusing extra service yet retaining his appearance as a committed Socialist. Candidates for

2

1 Construction soldiers in Prora, 1980s
2 A swearing-in ceremony in Leipzig, 1975

the Border Guard Division were also given a grilling. »If the imperialists were to launch an attack, would you hesitate in shooting?« The candidate pauses. »Both my schooling and my membership of the young pioneers have formed me into a peace-loving person. I cannot even begin to think that I could shoot at anyone«. That was the wrong answer. As the face of the Major turned crimson, the recruit could be sure he had just avoided serving on the border. After 1964, national servicemen in the DDR were given the choice between military service and serving in a construction battalion. Despite suffering considerable educational and professional discrimination, 27,000 young men chose to follow their conscience and served as so-called »construction soldiers« until 1989.

The conscription order came by post. Outlining the time and place of registration, it also specified what to bring: a bar of soap, shaving and sewing kit, cutlery, shoe cleaning equipment and toothpaste — all in duplicate. After collecting these items, the potential recruit had a haircut and bid his fond farewells. The next 18 months (or even three years) now consisted of marching, standing to attention, training and military cleanliness, interspersed with drunken singing and political instruction.

Returning to his family and friends on leave, the young soldier surprised those who knew him with the foreign jargon of soldiery. The most important thing he had to do on leave was to buy a tape measure. Back at the barracks, he cut off a centimetre a day, and on this covert calendar, counted the days until his service ended.

Erich Honecker
reviews troops, 1985

THE IMPOTENCE OF THE MIGHTY

It is certainly true, as many often repeat, that to concentrate on the Stasi is to ignore the factors which created the massive security apparatus in the first place. Nevertheless, the DDR would never have survived without the efforts of the Ministry for State Security. It may well have gathered masses of unnecessary information, wasting resources and man hours in the process, and it certainly created as many enemies as it actually faced. However, it was highly effective at making people feel very afraid. It was not just the visible world of uniforms, interrogations and prisons; the Stasi succeeded in creating a world of danger, doubt, mistrust and betrayal as ominous as it was invisible. Even the host of informants and tell-tales who served the machine assiduously were unaware how deep the tentacles of the Stasi reached.

The rumours of the perfidy of the system were legion and usually taken as being exaggerations. Consulting

the archives in 1990, people were astounded: not only were the rumours true, but proved tame in comparison to the actual situation as recorded in the files. Not subject to any form of legal control, the Stasi were able to open the post, force doctors to break confidentiality, place spies in all nature of relationships and force their way into any sphere of life in which they were interested. Not only did they break the law, they destroyed lives. Acting as police force, prosecu-

tor, judge, jury and legal oversight, the Stasi knew no bounds of law or morality in its quest to defend the system which had called it into being. Drilled to absolute obedience, the Stasi would have complied with any instruction issued by the Party. Utter paralysis suffered by the SED in 1989 meant that no orders were issued and the Stasi did nothing. This is the key event in the history of the DDR.

The MfS listening in

MFS TELEPHONE SURVEILLANCE IN THE DISTRICTS OF THE DDR, 1979–1985

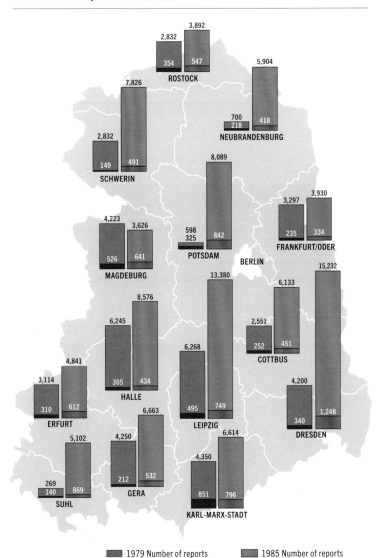

ROSTOCK 2,832 354 | 3,892 547

NEUBRANDENBURG 700 218 | 5,904 418

SCHWERIN 2,832 149 | 7,826 491

POTSDAM 598 325 | 8,089 842

BERLIN

MAGDEBURG 4,223 526 | 3,626 641

FRANKFURT/ODER 3,297 235 | 3,930 334

HALLE 6,245 305 | 8,576 434

COTTBUS 2,551 252 | 6,133 451

DRESDEN 4,200 340 | 15,232 1,248

LEIPZIG 6,268 495 | 13,380 749

ERFURT 3,114 310 | 4,841 612

GERA 4,250 212 | 6,663 532

SUHL 269 140 | 5,102 869

KARL-MARX-STADT 4,350 851 | 6,614 796

1979 Number of reports   1985 Number of reports
1979 Initiated measure   1985 Initiated measure

Photograph DDR Museum

GOOD COP, BAD COP

All those falling into the hands of the Stasi underwent a different experience and yet all tell an identical story. Having learnt their trade at a special University – the University of Applied Law – the MfS interrogators knew what to do to extract a confession. Pulling their victim out of their everyday routine, the victim was handcuffed, bundled into a waiting car and taken off to the local remand prison. Fingerprints and an odour sample were archived and the inmate was photographed from all angles. Taken to his cell, the prisoner began a very long wait. With no contact with the outside world, and no lawyer, the remand prisoner perched on his stool behind a window of glass bricks. Day turned to night and still he saw no-one, read nothing and heard nothing apart from a few short instructions. The prisoner was relieved to go to his interrogation. Led into a plain room with sound-isolated doors and a grille on the window, his interrogator asked him mockingly: »Do you know why you are here?« After the prisoner protested his innocence, the interrogator replied, »Socialist law enforcement doesn't make a habit of arresting innocent people«. The personal details were then recorded, twice, three times, ten times. Questions about the prisoner's private life, job, political views. Did you know about the flyers? Where did you obtain all that subversive literature? All interspersed with threats and insults. What do they know? What is important? The prisoner frets.

Then suddenly the interrogator is replaced. The second is much nicer. Would you like a cigarette? Coffee? It is easier to talk under such circumstances. Oh by the way, your wife has already given a full and open confession. He throws in a few intimate details. How do they know this? Did they have a bug in the house? Have they been opening my mail? Was there a spy? The textbook relationship of trust had been established after the third or even tenth interrogation. The Stasi man had been a good student – the prisoner tells him everything. After all, they know everything. If everybody has betrayed me, I don't need to worry about my friends. The case is passed on to the prosecution service. The Stasi operative is promoted.

»OFF TO BAUTZEN!«

The many public meetings held in that turbulent autumn of 1989 saw countless people unburdening themselves of the painful experiences of forty years. At one of the rallies, an older man told the crowd of his imprisonment for seditious comments. In his story of harassment, maltreatment, imprisonment in a pitch-black cell, hunger and forced labour, the most shocking aspect was his inability for twenty years to tell anyone — even his colleagues or family — what he had experienced. Once he started, the words just tumbled out — it was as though a spirit had left a well-sealed grave. His speech inserted a jarring note in the atmosphere of »dialogue« and many did not want to listen. The majority of East Germans — even the most critical — had turned a blind eye to the terror of the early DDR.

A practice of prisoner ransom began in later years of the SED system saw West Germany pay an average of just under 100,000 DM per person for a total of around 33,700 political prisoners. The true cost of such deals was silence. The beginning of détente between the two Germanys brought clear advantages, but also meant that the victims of the SED system were often ignored in West Germany.

Those released into the DDR also chose silence, as to talk would result in re-incarceration. Many were unable to believe the announcement after reunification that the East German state had held some 250,000 political prisoners; a figure which has been confirmed by the documents. In the 1970s and 1980s, the DDR held more than 3,000 political prisoners at any one time. The surprising aspect of this story is the silence within East German society on this subject during the 40 years of the state's existence. The most well-known prison in East Germany was Bautzen II, which housed a number of prominent dissidents and writers such as Walter Kempowski and Erich Loest, both of whom wrote books about their experiences. The phrase »off to Bautzen« soon entered the language. The existence and effects of further prisons such as Brandenburg, Cottbus, Bützow or the women's prison at Hoheneck entered the public consciousness only after reunification. Disrupting the widespread public evasion of such difficult subjects, former prisoners still experience difficulty in being heard. Nevertheless, any consideration of the DDR cannot ignore their stories.

THE FORBIDDEN DISTRICT

Stasi prisons were kept strictly secret. The Stasi Remand Centre in the Berlin district of Hohenschönhausen was located in a restricted area not marked on any map. Only Stasi employees lived in the surrounding streets. Prisoners never had any idea of where they were; if they were moved from one block to another, they were driven through Berlin for hours in order to change location by a few metres. They were even taken to other institutions to receive visits from family.

Side courtyard in the Central Remand Prison Berlin-Hohenschönhausen: an administrative building (right) and the prison hospital (left).

EAST MEETS WEST

For East Germans, a visit from friends or relatives from West Germany was a big day. For the visitor from the Capitalist West, it was an expression of family duty. After all, if you had the time and the money to fly to Thailand, why not drive the few miles over the East German border? On the other hand, it was much faster and easier to fly half way round the world to a different continent than it was to cross the German-German border. West Germans usually arrived in their car, which for East Germans was a sen-

Queue in front of an Intershop
in East Berlin in the 1980s

sation in itself. Watching the crowd
of young boys gawping in admiration
at this feat of West German engineering, SED members could only despair
at their lack of class consciousness.

East Germans expected gifts from
western visitors, but this posed its
own difficulties. Sugar and flour was
freely available in the DDR; a 100 DM
note would be appreciated, but it was
embarrassing. Conversation also
involved negotiating a number of

pitfalls: making fun of the surroundings would be taken as an insult, but then praising Socialism would only betray ignorance. After that, there was little more to say apart from bemoaning the perfidy of German-German division — but here both sides were in complete agreement.

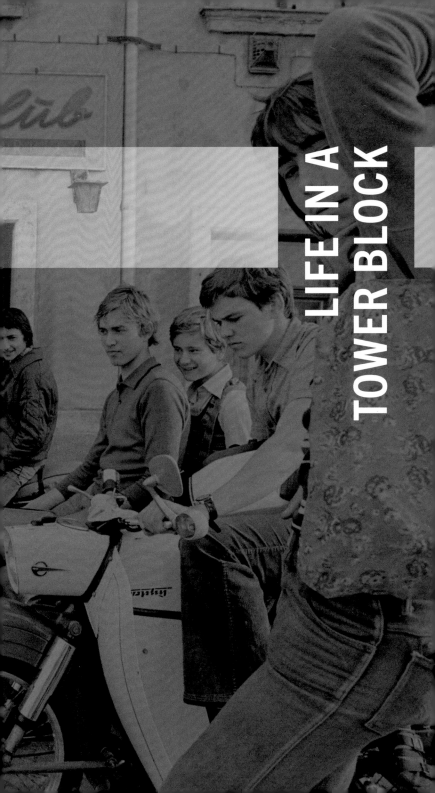

LIFE IN A
TOWER BLOCK

Gebrauchsanweisung
für Neubauwohnungen

VEB Wohnungsbaukombinat Cottbus

Sitz Hoyerswerda

Blessed was he who was issued with the keys to a flat in one of East Germany's new high-rise tower block estates. After all, they arrived after a very long time spent inching up the waiting lists; only marriage enabled people to jump the queue, and that was a spectacular step just to ensure that you could move out of your parents' home a little earlier. Having a place to sleep meant that the state viewed you as happy and not in need of a flat. Those taking possession of one of the prefabricated, uniform flats in the sky were bowled over by the unheard-of levels of luxury in which they could now wallow – central heating and a bath tub with hot and cold running water available day or night. Those living in pre-war housing could only dream of such comfort. The flat even came with an operating manual, a warranty and information about the communal areas on the estate. The leaflet exhorted the new householder to take care of the flat and even gave tips on the best way to wash the floor. Emergency information and civil defence instructions rounded off the booklet. The occupant was well-advised to look after his new flat – it had taken long enough to pay for the dwelling, and there was no money left for repairs or modernization.

ACCOMMODATION IN THE DDR

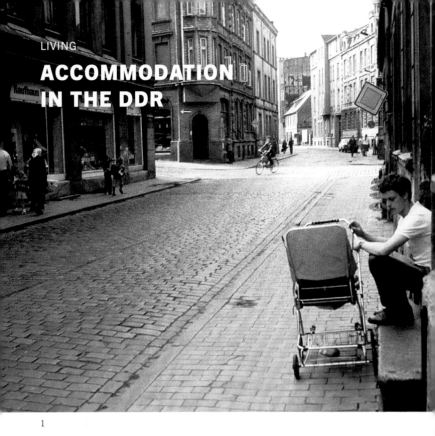

1

Any conversation between old friends meeting each other after a long time would at some point move towards the housing question. After all, the route to happiness in this matter was long and difficult. Housing was in short supply in the DDR, and modern housing even more so. The would-be householder had to submit an application, make repeated visits to the accommodation office and even search around to see if there was someone willing to swap. The reasons for the accommodation shortage were partly historical, partly financial. The arrival of a large number of refugees expelled from what had suddenly become Poland after 1945 had put pressure on regions which had been bombed into rubble. With little money to expand and repair

the housing stock, even the migration in the West before 1961 did little to ease the resulting pressure. Compounding this problem was the low rents charged for accommodation, which meant that parents had no incentive to move out of their flat once their children had left home. Often one old person was the only resident of a cavernous old flat.

In the 1980s, one in three households were housed in a crumbling residence dating back to before the Second World War. 1.7 million flats had no inside toilet, 1.3 million had no bath or shower. The majority of such old homes were heated with stoves, meaning coal had to be stored somewhere and carried in every day in winter. The countless

2

3

1 Old housing, 1985
2 A new house in Arnstadt, 1974
3 Post-war housing in Lehmbruckstraße,
Berlin 1959

smoking chimneys made for dirt and grime. With no means and no incentive to repair their flats and houses, the inhabitants of pre-war accommodation had to watch whilst their surroundings decayed. Cities like Görlitz and Leipzig looked like scenes out of a horror film.

With the official priorities of the 1970s set to »quick and cheap«, town planners concentrated on erecting standardized and prefabricated high-rise tower block flats. By 1988, these estates made up one third of the DDR's housing stock. With between three and four people allocated three rooms (plus kitchen and bathroom) with an average floorspace of 67 m^2, the new flats were very small by modern standards.

Hanging out the washing in front
of a tower block, Wurzen 1980s

Although a little more expensive than the average, they were still affordable.

The final third of the nation lived in flats built between 1945 and 1970. Few people were able to build a new house of their own. Although some 32 per cent of flats were owner-occupied, the difficulties of obtaining materials and very complicated red tape meant that only a few houses were built between 1960 and 1989. The period after 1990 saw a major upswing in building and an even greater programme of modernization. Today, the once decaying urban centres of the DDR are truly a sight to behold.

»A HOME FOR ALL«

1

The unification of economic and social policy announced by Erich Honecker in 1972 meant that East Germans could finally start enjoying a greater level of private consumption. Those who worked hard now expected to enjoy the fruits of their labour. The clearest expression of this change was the new house-building programme started in 1973. Concentrating on the industrial prefabrication of large high-rise housing units meant that much more housing could be built faster and more cheaply. Plans called for three million flats to be built by 1990, but Erich Honecker was only able to announce the completion of the three-millionth flat in 1988 by massaging the statistics.

The most common form of tower block flat populating the new housing estates now popping up across East Germany was the »Wohnungsbauserie 70«, otherwise known as the WBS 70.

2

1 The construction of a 11-storey
tower block in Marzahn (Berlin), 1980
2 WBS tower blocks in Neubrandenburg,
1976

A particular feature was the variability which this series allowed: the unitary façade could be varied through the application of different types of balcony, windows and even artistic design elements. Although tenants were delighted finally to move into a flat with hot and cold running water, a bathroom and central heating, they still found the estates to be dull, uniform and just a little soul-destroying. Some of the new residents even started to try and swap flats, so that they could return to the older stone and tile housing in the city centre. The flats may not have been as comfortable, but at least life was more varied there.

NUMBER OF WBS 70 FLATS CONSTRUCTED

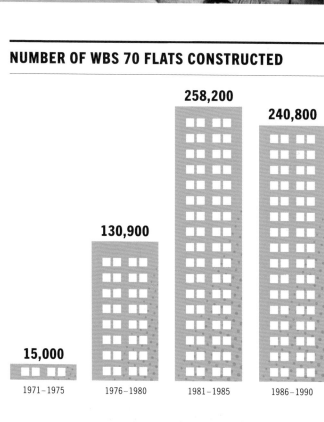

15,000

130,900

258,200

240,800

1971–1975   1976–1980   1981–1985   1986–1990

LIFE IN A TOWER BLOCK

The »Carat« storage unit made by »VEB Polstermöbel Sebnitz« was the centre-piece of every living room. A standardized product designed to fit into every standardized high-rise flat, the ubiquity of the model made for dull viewing. Visitors to almost any household in the DDR could safely bet that they would encounter this familiar storage solution. Although the furniture system could be extended by the addition of further (rather expensive) elements, the number of combinations was finite.

Although the product of state-of-the-art East German design, the furniture range was manufactured with an old-fashioned elm-wood appearance. In essence, the designers were giving their customers what they wanted — functional furniture with a traditional, or even kitschy appearance. More importantly however, »Carat« fulfilled its function, providing a lot of space for the usual assortment of possessions collected over a lifetime.

CELEBRATING SOCIALIST STYLE

Socialism liked to celebrate its people and institutions: The Day of the Child; The Day of the National People's Army; The Day of the Metalworkers; there was even a Day of the Postal and Communications Workers. The most important of these days however was 1 May and the celebrations for the birth of the Republic on 7 October, which were accompanied by a plethora of parades, speeches and waving. Celebrated with-out the official Socialist pathos, regions had their own traditional litany of folk festivals and families continued to mark birthdays, weddings, the first day at school and even Christmas and Easter in the traditional manner. The state had nothing against a good party, it did however worry about providing the required volumes of sparkling wine and cake. The SED also tried to police the content of private celebrations, with a campaign to replace Christian festivals such as confirmation and first communion with the Coming of Age Ceremony.

Nevertheless, nearly every family got together to celebrate Christmas and Easter, with tree, song and presents.

Whatever occasion was being marked, alcohol was never far from the hands of the revellers. In the 1980s, East Germans drank an average of ten litres of pure alcohol in the form of beer, which given the lack of state regulations – the DDR abandoned the traditional German law regulating alcohol quality (the famous »Reinheitsgebot«) – meant that every beer could provide a surprise. Not just a nation of beer drinkers, the average East German also imbibed a range of much stronger beverages. Indeed, able to choose from promising names such as »Goldi«, »Primasprit« or the »Blue Strangler« it is unsurprising that they often turned to the bottle. The only places where alcohol consumption was forbidden were on the road and in the army. Motorists could sweeten their journey with the alcohol-free beer »Aubi«. It might have improved their driving skills, but did not taste good.

Mother and child celebrating Christmas,
Berlin 1965

141

PER CAPITA CONSUMPTION BEER (litres)

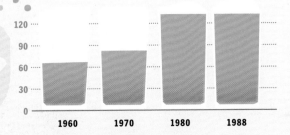

	1960	1970	1980	1988

PER CAPITA CONSUMPTION WINE (litres)

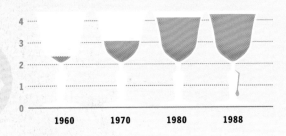

	1960	1970	1980	1988

PER CAPITA CONSUMPTION SPIRITS (litres)

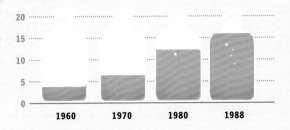

	1960	1970	1980	1988

1

1 Brass band playing at the Erfurt festival celebrating
the 32nd anniversary of the DDR, 7.10.1981
2 A housewarming party at the Wachter family from
the series: »The People of Erlln«, 1983

2

BOOKWORMS UNDER CENSORSHIP

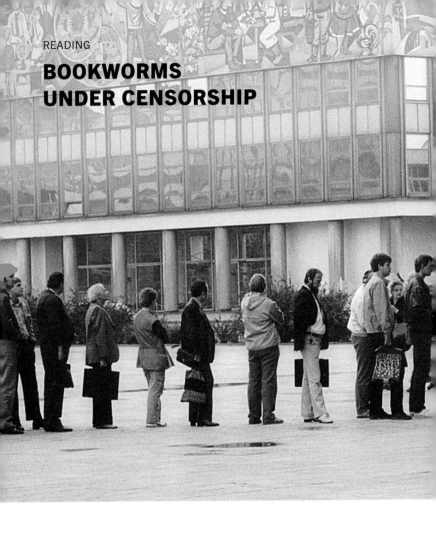

The DDR was proud to call itself a »land of readers«, pointing to the large print runs of »quality literature« in East German publishing houses. As with all statistics, however, the truth had to be read between the lines.

A total of 6,073 titles were published in the DDR in 1989, which was in line with the level of the year before. West German publishers, on the other hand, issued a staggering 65,680 titles.

Photograph DDR Museum

The queue for the bookshop
»The good Book« (»Das gute Buch«)
in Berlin, 1985

Despite coming off poorly in this comparison, East Germany was nonetheless a nation of bookworms, not least because the Party encouraged high levels of literacy in schools. In the 1950s, Party bosses never tired of exhorting the working class to »storm the heights of culture«. Once arrived on these sunlit uplands however, the average reader found that they were presented with a heavily-censored selection of literature, even of the writings from the Socialist brother states. The literary tastes of the Party had also advanced little since the 1920s. Nevertheless, East German thirst for cosmopolitan literature raged unquenched. If they were forbidden from travelling to London, Paris or Barcelona, at least they could read Dickens or Hemmingway. Despite large print runs of licensed copies, books were always in short supply in the DDR; the best reads were only ever available »under the counter«.

145

MONOPOLY
MORE THAN JUST A GAME

Games may appear to be nothing more than a simple pastime, but the SED decided that it even needed to police the realms of fantasy. No more than a very popular piece of fun, the SED reviled »Monopoly« as the propaganda instrument of a rapacious imperialist Capitalism which sought to capture young minds and pervert them onto the paths to acquisitiveness. A good Socialist nation such as the DDR could not tolerate the existence of such a game and confiscated all specimens of it coming in the post from West Germany. As ever, what is forbidden becomes attractive and many families simply constructed their own version. The resulting cornucopia of homemade fun certainly started on the premise of the world-famous game, but soon involved idiosyncratic extensions. This served to make the games even more fun and more popular. Not for the first time, the Party had shot itself in the foot.

The version of Monopoly in our exhibition was designed and made by Axel Frankenberg from Aschersleben in 1985. His version of the game did not revolve around the building of hotels, but the acquisition and maintenance of good vehicles.

WATCHING THE CLASS ENEMY

As a rule, electromagnetic waves do not stop at international borders to have their passports stamped. As such, the invention of television gave the East-West conflict an especially interesting twist. Whilst the SED tried to wall in its citizens on all sides, all the people had to do to get into contact with the West was to switch on their televisions and watch. The only solution to this conundrum would have been for the DDR to offer the better television programmes. Many of the films made by East German studios — especially literary adaptations of Hans Fallada or Theodor Fontane — were undoubtedly of a very high quality, whilst the Monday evening showings of UFA films produced during the Third Reich continued to attract large audiences.

Seeking to profit from this captive audience, the SED sent their chief propagandist Karl-Eduard von Schnitzler into the fray, giving him a transmission slot directly after the films. Presenting a programme called »The Black Channel«, he showed small clips from West German television, which he commented on from the perspective of Marxism-Leninism, often pointing out things which were usually impossible to see from any other angle. In short order, he became the most hated figure on East German television.

News programmes in the East German media were also terrible. The language was wooden, the reports were usually dull and were invariably ridiculous in their one-sidedness. The most off-putting aspect of the news was the toe-curling obsequiousness of tone adopted by the reporters. Always making sure to name every word of the mile-long titles borne by Socialist decision-makers, even the dullest of news stories took up considerable time. In consequence, even the most fervent Socialists tuned in to West German television, if they wanted to know what was going on in the world without being bored to tears. The only area in which reception of West German TV was not possible was the area around Dresden, and it became known as the »Valley of the Clueless«. Happy that at least one part of their Republic was cloistered from the lies of imperialism, the Stasi were at a loss to understand why the inhabitants of Dresden committed the highest number of ideological crimes. It was perhaps because they lacked the safety valve of watching Capitalism, which for the majority of East Germans made up for not being able to visit it in person. The greatest achievement of the western media was the maintenance of a joint national identity of language and culture. German re-unification was forged on the airwaves.

TEMPO PEAS
TEMPO IN THE KITCHEN

The technicians of the 1960s decided that the poor overworked housewives of the DDR should be given a helping hand in the kitchen. Moreover, the East German woman was officially emancipated, and her labour was needed in the factories. In addition to a range of electrical household goods, the use of ready meals was to bring a tasty solution to familiar problems. Peter Kretschmer, a scientist at the Rehbrücke Institute for Cereal Processing was tasked with shortening the cooking process for dried peas, which needed soaking over days and cooking for a long time. A year later he had pioneered a procedure to dry leguminous vegetables under high pressure. They could now be cooked and served in ten minutes. Tempo peas! The principle was later extended to produce a range of high-speed delicacies such as »Tempo beans«, »Tempo lentils« and quick cooking rice. These convenience foods are still available for purchase in supermarkets and even made a starring appearance in the feature film »Goodbye Lenin«. Whatever their success, they did nothing to break down traditional gender roles.

TEMPO PEAS

- Manufacturer: »VEB Nahrungsmittelwerke Suppina«, Auerbach
- Other related products: Tempo beans, Tempo lentils, a range of soups
- Package size: 250 g.
- Price: 0.60 Marks
- Made from 1969, continued by ACO GmbH & Co. KG

LET MUTTI HAVE A GO!

The DDR constitution from 1949 conferred identical legal and political rights on both men and women. Not just seeking to build on the legacy of the Weimar constitution of 1919, East German planners saw the need to mobilize female labour for the ailing East German economy. The goal of maximising the workforce was to be facilitated by providing universal child care and by making improvements in household technology. Despite such aims, traditional gender roles retained their sway over East German society. In 1970, women performed 37.1 hours of the average 47.1 hours of domestic chores. They were also responsible for taking the children to kindergarten or school, accompanying them to doctor's appointments and going shopping. The one-year parental leave may also have been made available to men in 1986, but the statutory one day off every month to perform housework was reserved exclusively for women.

The 1960s saw a few beggarly attempts to encourage men to take up dusting and hoovering, but little changed. Women worked hard at home and did not make much progress at work, often working below their level

1

of qualification and earning less than men for performing a comparable professional role. More women worked in traditionally male-dominated occupations than in the West, but the majority of women still performed low-paid work in the service sector. There were very few female managers and politicians, and absolutely no women in the Politburo. East German women did not obtain social equality with their male counterparts, although they were looked after nicely once a year on 8 March: International Women's Day.

2

1 Gender roles in the kitchen, 1976
2 A female crane operator, Zwickau 1981

WOMEN IN MANAGEMENT POSITIONS, 1988

 POLITICS
1 minister

 **UNIVERSITY**
15 %
of university lecturers

 THE SOCIAL SERVICES
52 %
of the group leaders

 INDUSTRY
2.4 %
of state combine directors

 TRADES
20 %
of master tradespersons

NET EARNINGS IN COMPARISON, 1988

819
Marks

585
Marks

A LIFE BETWEEN SHORTAGE AND GLUTTONY

»We're out« was the standard reply to many inquiries in a shop. Although the basics of everyday life were usually — but not always — readily available, the planned economy was exceptionally bad at meeting demand for more complicated needs. This necessitated buying what was on offer to store for the future. Fresh produce had to be cooked, then frozen or dried. A typical family larder was stuffed to bursting with conserved food. It was the only way to ensure a varied diet.

PER CAPITA CONSUMPTION
BEEF (in kg)

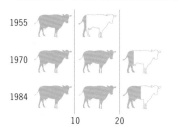

1955

1970

1984

10   20

PER CAPITA CONSUMPTION
PORK (in kg)

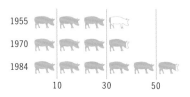

1955

1970

1984

10   30   50

Traditional German cooking — plenty of meat supplemented by carbohydrates — lived on in the DDR. The familiar range of sausages and the ever-reliable potato were joined by the product of industrial poultry farming: a broiled chicken, named the »Goldbroiler«. The political supremacy of the Soviet Union also had its culinary impact with the import of »Solyanka«, a thick, spicy meat soup which soon established itself on the East German culinary scene. The 1980s also saw the introduction of East German ver-

Photograph DDR Museum

Photograph DDR Museum

PER CAPITA CONSUMPTION
CHICKEN (in kg)

1955

1970

1984

4   8

sions of American fast food: the »Ketwurst (a combination of the word ketchup and sausage), »Grilletta« (the East German for Hamburger) and »Krusta« (a variation on the pizza). Combined with the lack of fresh fruit and vegetables available in the DDR, this emu-

lation of Capitalist eating practices contributed to the general paucity of the East German diet, but strangely enough only the East German women – but not their menfolk – exhibited greater levels of obesity.

PER CAPITA CONSUMPTION
FRUIT (in kg)

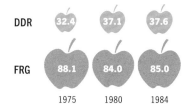

DDR   32.4   37.1   37.6

FRG   88.1   84.0   85.0

1975   1980   1984

ADOLESCENT OBESITY, 1984

DDR

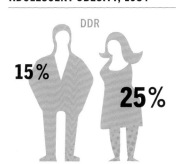

15%

25%

FRG

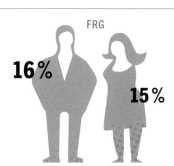

16%

15%

HEALTH FOR ALL!

All workers had equal access to healthcare through their standardized statutory social insurance. This meant that a Social Security card was a well-guarded treasure providing access to medical treatment and rest-cures as well as accident insurance and an old age pension. Nonetheless, and despite all the official propaganda, an East German patient was not as well cared for as his West German counterpart. Lacking medicines and equipment, East German hospitals provided 24 doctors and 98 beds for every 10,000 patients. Outpatient centres had a single doctor to treat 808 citizens. The situation was even worse for those with toothache – one dentist had to treat 1,383 patients. The claims made of comprehensive treatment were nothing short of a lie.

Aware of this situation, the authorities placed their hope in the old adage that prevention is better than a cure. Routine screening programmes were rolled out in childcare centres and continued well into adulthood. Despite spending half of its budget on prophylaxis, the healthcare system was still overstretched.

NUMBER OF EMPLOYEES IN THE HEALTH CARE SECTOR

	1970	1980	1987	1989 (until 30.9.1989)
Doctors	27,255	33,894	40,516	41,544
Dentists	7,349	9,709	12,527	12,804
Pharmacists	2,885	3,549	4,049	4,342
Nurses	–	98,500	103,500	–

A polyclinic in Berlin-Prenzlauer Berg, 1986

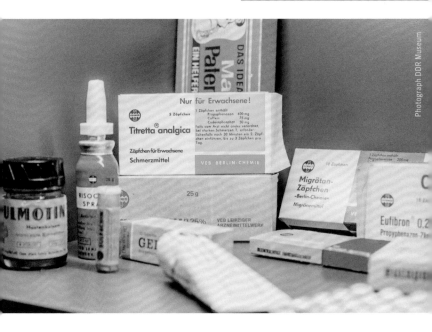

THE OVERALL
FOR JOB AND HOUSEHOLD

A key element of female clothing in the DDR was the overall. From housewives to the lady farmer, no self-respecting East German woman did without these practical, hard-wearing and exceptionally brightly-coloured garments made of polyamide fibres. They were so popular that many men even took the plunge and put them on. After all, they were easy to wash and protected your good clothes from all manner of dirt. They were also available in any number of colours and designs. Although similar to Nylon or Perlon, as it was made in the DDR, national pride dictated that the material be named DeDeRon. The chemicals revolution of the 1960s — as every good East German knew, »chemistry brings bread, prosperity and beauty« — meant that clothes made from Dederon were affordable, hard wearing and above all, highly colourful. The same material was used for coats, bags and stockings. The only drawback to these sartorial masterpieces was the fact that they made the wearer sweat profusely. Although they were very popular in the DDR, it is unclear just why they have come to symbolize Socialist Germany. After all, such items were just as popular in the West.

SIBYLLE'S PROMISE

The ancient Greeks called female oracles Sybille. The most popular fashion magazine in the DDR was also called »Sibylle«, but her predictions tended to be somewhat unrealistic. Showing modern, fashionable, state-of-the-art clothing, it ignored the reality of supply — such clothes existed nowhere in the DDR. The East German fashion industry wanted both to distance itself from western fashion, with its fleeting fads, and produce hard-wearing and practical clothing suited to the needs of working women. Nevertheless, the »Berlin Fashion Institute« never succeeded in creating a new aesthetic

The outfit »Lorraine« presented at the Leipzig Autumn fair, 1966

and at best, managed to copy western fashion. Hampered by the heavily bureaucratic planned economy, the East German fashion industry often found itself designing a world-beating collection (so it believed) only to find that they could not produce the clothes fast enough. The supply of materials also dictated large-scale changes to their designs, reducing them to the aesthetic minimum. What clothes the designers managed to produce were sold at high prices in the Socialist boutique chain »Exquisit«.

A new SED dictum from the 1960s also influenced fashion: »chemistry brings bread, prosperity and beauty«. The high price of cotton and the necessity of its import forced East German clothing manufacturers to depend on the use of artificial fibres. Uninspired, synthetic clothing of poor quality did not enthuse the fashion-conscious citizen. Those with West German relatives waited for gifts, those without made do and mended. At least »Sibylle« helped those ready to help themselves, providing a range of sewing patterns. She may have promised much, but it was the reader that had to deliver.

Photograph DDR Museum

Fashion made of the artificial fibre »Grisuten«
bearing the name »Youth 73« (»Jugend 73«)
presented at the Leipzig Autumn fair, 1972

LOVE, SEX AND A MARRIAGE LOAN

Rumour had it that East German marital bliss was more fun that its Capitalist counterpart. Historians interested in this sort of thing have also come to the same conclusion. Statistics indicate that East Germans lost their virginity earlier, married younger and had more children. Nevertheless, a range of factors, including widespread use of the contraceptive pill – known in the DDR as the »planned child pill« – after 1965 meant that East German mothers matched their western counterparts in having fewer children. The fall in birth rates alarmed the state, which set about trying to encourage couples to start a family.

Young married couples were given preferential treatment when it came to allocating accommodation and received an interest-free »marriage loan«. Women were also granted a year's maternity leave, after which they were able to return to their job; pregnant women and breast-feeding mothers were granted flexible working hours and could later count on universal childcare. This all served to reduce the speed with which the birth rate fell, but female independence and easy access to divorce played their part in reducing the stability of marriage.

A youth disco at the beginning of the 1980s

DIVORCES IN THE DDR (TOTAL NUMBERS)

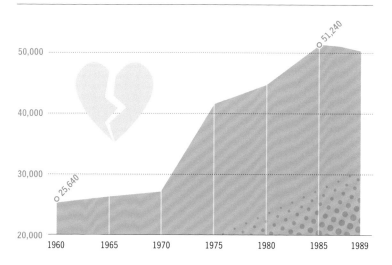

50,000

40,000

30,000

○ 25,640

20,000

○ 51,240

1960   1965   1970   1975   1980   1985   1989

AVERAGE NUMBER OF CHILDREN PER WOMAN

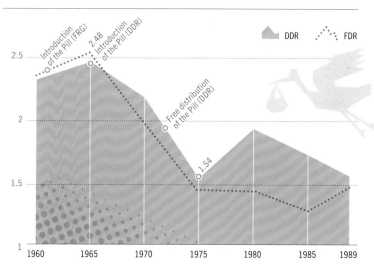

Introduction
of the Pill (FRG)

2.48

Introduction
of the Pill (DDR)

Free distribution
of the Pill (DDR)

1.54

2.5

2

1.5

1

DDR   ⋰ FDR

1960   1965   1970   1975   1980   1985   1989

He was so sweeeet! Pittiplatsch — Pitti for short — the television goblin advanced to become a cult figure amongst East German toddlers, who repeated his favourite catchphrases constantly. Bold and cheeky, Pitti liked making up tall tales, eating pancakes and resisting all attempts to send him to bed. Running through an astounding 3,000 episodes from 1962–1991, his career exhibited a remarkable level of flexibility. Starting life in a tailor's workshop, he later featured in another long-running children's favourite, the Sandman. Wherever children met him, he was usually accompanied by a dog called Moppi and Gabble the duck. Gabble was a good duck, but just a little precocious. Although she never tired of telling Pitti to behave himself and to eat fewer sweets, she was in fact a very loyal friend. Anyway, Pitti was the star and could get away with anything. After all, his heart was in the right place — he never did anything seriously wrong and could usually win over his rather goody-goody friend with his charm and humour. All in all, not a bad role model for life in the Socialist state.

THE IMAGINATION KNOWS NO BOUNDS

The characters of a good children's book stay with us for the rest of our lives. Those growing up in East Germany were no different and followed the fate of favourite characters avidly: would Aunt Koschka emerge unscathed from the burning ruins of her wonderful house? The children read on to find out. East Germany published so much top-quality children's literature that it could do without some of the acknowledged classics, and for reasons known only to the SED, Karl May was frowned on until 1982. Children could also read about the miracles worked by the Red Army, the adventures of underground anti-fascist fighters and the heroes who built Socialism, but few did. Although the state wanted to use children's literature to form Socialist personalities, the publishing industry took any chance to keep the flame of older traditions alive within the context of the new system. Attracting top authors, illustrators and editors, East German publishing houses were responsible for producing some masterpieces of German literature.

Puss in Boots from Werner Klemke's
»Grimm's Fairy Tales«, 1963

173

THE YOUTHFUL STATE

»The world is so good when you are young / we are working for a new, young world« were the optimistic lyrics to one FDJ song. Whatever the likelihood of this happening, it was clear that the SED was not really doing very much to achieve this aim. The Party knew that it needed to buy the support of the younger generation, and was careful to ensure that university study was free-of-charge. Many students were even given grants, and all guaranteed a job after graduation. Such opportunities carried their own cost however: the state expected political reliability.

The DDR was based on a paradox. Seeking to create a new future, the Party called on its youth to come up with new ideas regarding the best path to a better tomorrow. On the other hand, the old men running the government feared anything new and did their best to make sure that young people just did as they were told. The main areas of conflict centred on the areas of music and fashion. Wanting greater freedom of experimentation, young people took advantage of a small window of opportunity – 1956, the early 1960s or 1971 – to gain concessions, only to flinch as the state then started to claw back what it had only recently granted. The state, however, wanted to control everything and smelled political unreliability in every call for better music and nicer clothes. Not to be discouraged, each subsequent generation discovered what is perhaps a deeper truth – the attempt to make one's own way in life is often the most fulfilling. When young, everything is great. Perhaps the song was not wrong after all.

East German youths in the 1980s

176

»SKR 700«
LISTENING TO THE WEST

A number of former East Germans wrote to the museum highlighting the absence from our exhibition of the cassette recorder »SKR 700«. Often presented to adolescents to mark the occasion of their Coming of Age Ceremony, many used it to record music played on western radio stations. Costing 1,540 Marks, the recorder was not cheap, but it was still affordable if the whole family clubbed together. Although the sound was only suitable for home use, it came in stereo and the two aerials meant that the listener had a good reception. Most importantly, the recording was always good. Designed by Toshiba and made under license in the DDR, the model was very kind to the tapes, and pulled them apart much less often than its predecessor models. Perhaps that's why the »SKR 700« was also successfully exported to the West.

BEAT MUSIC
BY COMMITTEE

For a long time, the SED set its face against the cultural dominance of western beat music amongst the young, but in 1970, the Party bowed to the inevitable and allowed it to be played in the DDR. What previously had been decried as an expression of western decadence and the agent of imperialist propaganda, was now unleashed on the ears of young Socialists. The advent of East German bands singing in German made this new music form appear safer. Groups with names such as »The Puhdys« and »Silly« advanced to cult status during this decade, only to fall out of favour ten years later. In the late 1980s, everything English was »in«; East German bands were »out«. This was not simply due to disenchantment with the political system; the quality of the German bands had also fallen. Every aspiring guitar band was forced to audition in front of a state committee, which issued permits to play at concerts. Unfortunately, wherever the fingers of the committee members were located, it was not on the pulse of youth, and they issued permits to those who could play well, but did not enthuse the record-buying public.

After 1990, East Rock was »out« again, only to enjoy a renaissance in the mid-1990s. Bands like »Silly« currently enjoy a considerable following amongst former East Germans; the only bands from the East to make it big in both East and West were those who did not emphasize their roots. The hard rockers from »Rammstein« are a good example of this phenomenon.

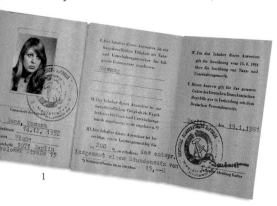

1

1 »License for public performance« issued to Tamara Danz, 1987
2 The Puhdys playing at the »Rock for Peace« held at the Palace of the Republic in Berlin, 1986
3 A single from »The Sputniks«, 1964

Rhythmus für junge Leute

Gitarren-Twist
Theme For Young Lovers

Amiga

Bestell-Nr. 4 50 443

Die
Sputniks
mit
dem
modernen
Gitarren-
Sound

2

3

179

THE PATH OF LIFE

East German restaurants were always full, but never more so than on the Sunday afternoons before and after Easter. Having just attended the Socialist »Coming of Age Ceremony« (»Jugendweihe«), legions of well-dressed families now set course for restaurants in which they had reserved a table, often months in advance. The »Jugendweihe« had been conducted in a local hall and involved a ceremony at which oaths were said, and the newly minted adults were presented with a special book, a bouquet of flowers and a quote saying something worthy. Having arrived in the eateries, the day was rounded off with gifts, much food and perhaps even the first official taste of alcohol.

What was later viewed as rather kitschy began life as the focus of a rumbustious conflict between Church and

State. The »Coming of Age Ceremony« was a Socialist innovation dating back to the 19th century, developed as an alternative to Confirmation or the First Communion. Revived in the DDR in 1955, the first oath which the children swore was not especially Socialist, yet still provoked clerical outrage. Piqued at the challenge to their authority, the Churches decreed that children opting for such a ritual would not be allowed to participate in the more ancient church rites. Only a massive campaign by the SED and FDJ ensured that some 17.7 per cent of schoolchildren took part in the new ceremony, a proportion which only increased in 1958. After that, by 1988, participation in the secular ritual increased until some 97.3 per cent of all children opted for this path into adulthood. Where the Party might once have celebrated, they now saw that mass participation had watered down any claim to Socialist purity. The Churches had also made their peace with the dual path to adulthood. The Church authorities knew that children not attending the Socialist ceremony would experience difficulty in gaining admission to a higher school, and they wanted to spare their parents the conflict of conscience. What had begun as preparation for a lifetime of commitment to Socialism had become yet another ritual of empty pathos.

1 Giving the pledge at the Coming of Age ceremony held in the House of Culture at »VEB Bergmann-Borsig«, 1987
2 Participants in Coming of Age ceremonies held between 1983 and 1989 were presented with this book.

Vom Sinn unseres Lebens

Bearing the magnificent title »HBM 250 Multimax DIY Drill Pistol« (»Heimwerker-Bohrpistole HBM 250 Multimax«), the »HBM 250« was more than just an electric drill, with accessories to transform it into a hammer drill, circular saw, jigsaw and sanding machine. With a bit of imagination, it could also morph into a hedge trimmer. Given the context of the tasks that the average DDR householder was required to perform however and the impossibility of finding a tradesman to do them, this little feat of engineering became a vital piece of equipment, exerting an influence on the life of its owner far exceeding its size and price. The only drawback was the short length of its power cable. Just how long were those hedges?

This life-enhancing tool came in two versions. The standard model, designed in 1963 by Wolfgang Dyroff was available for only 123.70 Marks

and was manufactured by a number of companies including »VEB Elektrowerkzeuge und Apparate Sebnitz«. Not speed-controlled, it was not produced in large numbers. The 250 Watt, speed-controlled model was much more expensive,

but then it was able to perform a whole range of tasks. The only challenge was presented by its chronic unreliability. A later development was the »Smalcalda« drill. This orange device gave a higher performance, but was much more expensive. Since it didn't provide any additional functionality compared to the cheaper models, the average East German consumer saw no reason to buy it. In the DDR, »new« was often just a code for »much more expensive«.

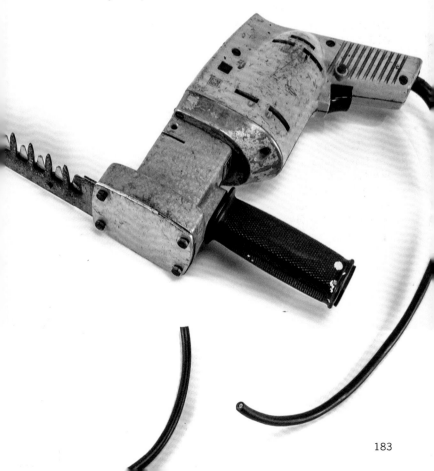

A HOBBYIST'S PARADISE

A Trabant P50 in front of its garage, 1958

»Necessity is the mother of invention«.
»Self-help is the best help«. Although
platitudes, these proverbs nonetheless describe the reality of life at home

in the DDR. Plagued by an acute shortage of materials and spare parts, the average East German householder was thrown back on his own resources and needed to beg, borrow, collect and appropriate what he needed. Once acquired, these treasures of everyday life were squirreled away and guarded jealously. The family cellar or shed, functioning both as home to this collection and site of invention, often witnessed great feats of amateur engineering, out of which emerged seriously improvised yet longlasting solutions to a range of everyday challenges.

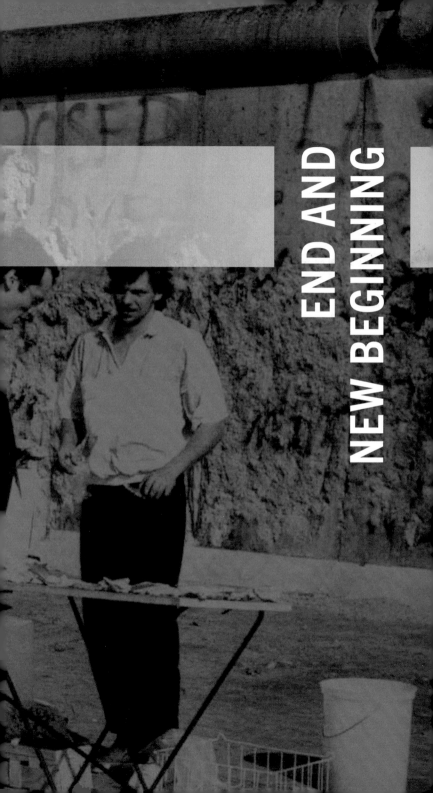

END AND
NEW BEGINNING

THE PEACEFUL UPRISING

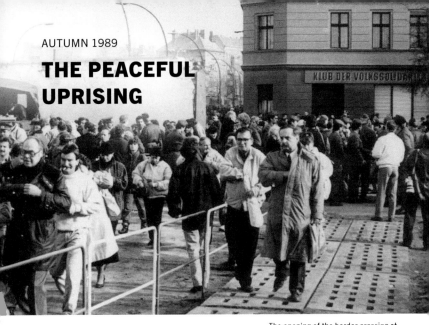

The opening of the border crossing at Bernauer Straße, 11.11.1989

The DDR turned forty on 7 October 1989, and the massed ranks of international guests and the diplomatic corps all congregated in the Palace of the Republic to celebrate its birthday. Whilst the champagne flowed in the Parliament buildings, the general public celebrated on the Alexanderplatz with brass bands and sausages. This façade of Socialist normality covered a much more volatile reality. Those not trying to escape via Prague or Budapest stayed at home to discuss how things should best be changed. The birthday celebrations of 7 October amounted to a wake. A large group of people on the Alexanderplatz began at 5 o`clock a prearranged demonstration, demanding freedom and democracy. Observed by Stasi cameras, something inconceivable, something inconceivable began to unfold: an anti-state demonstration in the heart of the capital. Waiting until Gorbachev had left for Moscow, the state now unleashed its waiting henchmen who beat back the crowds with brute force. The turning point came two days later, as 70,000 people gathered in Leipzig to demand democratic reform. Overwhelmed by the sheer size of the masses, the authorities hesitated to give the order to disperse the crowds: the people had seized back power with their peaceful protest. There was no turning back. People gathered across the Republic to take a stand. Everything that followed in the ensuing months was the result of this decision to protest. A lot did follow – the wall fell, the regional Stasi outposts were occupied and the central Stasi headquarters was stormed. With the first democratic elections held on 18 March 1990, it was not long until the reunification of the two Germanies on 3 October. One of the most radical of revolutions was concluded within a year without a single shot being fired.

TURNING THIS SHIP AROUND OR A PEACEFUL REVOLUTION?

Raised on the violent stories of 1789 and 1918/19, East Germans initially did not think of calling the overthrow of the SED a revolution: the mass demonstrations of Autumn 1989 remained entirely peaceful. Instead, they preferred to speak of »die Wende«, a term usually used to indicate a »turn in events« or »turning around in traffic«. What most people forget was that the term was coined by Egon Krenz, the last strong-man of the DDR and no democrat. Speaking to the Central Committee of the SED, the inner circle of the dictatorship, he promised: »With today's meeting, we aim to regain the political and ideological upper hand«. Krenz certainly wanted to change course, but ultimately the ship was supposed to keep sailing in the same overall direction and be steered by the same crew and captain.

The term »peaceful revolution« is really only suitable for politicians giving big speeches or in books written by historians for other historians. Nevertheless, it probably accurately captures the character of the events of 1989/90, which remains to this day the largest ever political change brought about without bloodshed. A highly-armed and potentially violent state apparatus was brought to its knees without any violence and with no retribution. This is the true achievement of the East German population, of which they can be rightly proud.

Demonstrators on the Alexanderplatz holding a banner with a caricature of Egon Krenz, East Berlin 4.11.1989

With the exception of the early stage of Socialist monumentalism, East German architecture was more or less utilitarian in character. This is not to say, however, that the SED had no taste for art; the Party commissioned a number of frescos to enliven the urban cityscape. One such was the work »In Praise of Communism« by Roland Paris. Presented to the authorities in 1969, it was immediately hidden away in the Office for Statistics, as the end result was not as celebratory as the SED had original-

ly intended. Closer study of this monumental piece of art is instructive, as it is representative of the attempt of many of the dissidents in the 1960s to use the framework of Marxism to critique the realities of the DDR. Added to this was the expressionist style — the SED were displeased.

Based on official propaganda, the tryptic works from left to right with a depiction redolent of the last judgement and the battle between good and evil. The central position conventionally reserved for the

MURAL
IN PRAISE OF COMMUNISM

redeemer is occupied by five Red Army soldiers and a woman pushed into the background. A Red flag replaces the halo. Evil is incarnate as a being half man half shark clothed in the garb of a West German Capitalist. The exploited masses on one third of the picture are struggling towards freedom under the leadership of the Party and headed by Karl Liebknecht. To the far right is the sun-lit Communist utopia with its high-rise blocks of flats, technical progress and children playing together.

As the building of the former House of Statistics was demolished in 2010, the DDR Museum was only too pleased to purchase and restore the mural, putting it on public display for the first time.

CHRONOLOGY

1945
End of the Second World War. Expropriation of land owners in the Soviet zone and the nationalization of large-scale industry.

1946
Forced amalgamation of the Communist Party of Germany (KPD) and the Social Democratic Party of Germany (SPD) to form the Socialist Unity Party of Germany (SED).

1948
The Soviet blockade of West Berlin. America and Great Britain supply West Berlin by air for 11 months.

1949
7 October: foundation of the DDR (German Democratic Republic).

The East German television makes its first transmission.

1950
First election to the DDR Parliament. Voters can accept or reject the SED-led »United List of the National Front«. The number of seats in Parliament awarded to the parties is arranged in advance.

1952

The second Party Conference of the SED announces the construction of Socialism. Prices and working norms are increased. The establishment of the People's Police in Barracks (KVP) marks the start of the militarization of East German society.

1953

17 June: strikes and demonstrations in over 700 cities and smaller towns. Soviet tanks crush the protests.

1955

First edition of »Mosaik«, a well-known East German comic book.

The first official Coming of Age Ceremonies are performed at Easter.

1956

»Destalinization« in the Soviet Union. The Hungarian Uprising. Protests in East German universities.

Establishment of the National People's Army (NVA).

1957

Show trials of critical intellectuals end with long prison sentences.

The first Trabant P 50 is produced.

1958

The fifth SED Party Conference announces the »Ten Commandments of Socialist Morality«.

The end of rationing.

Announcement of the 60/40 directive: 60 % of music played at all concerts and other public events must have been composed and produced in the Eastern bloc.

1960

»The Socialist Spring in the Countryside« brings the collectivization of agriculture and the first crisis in the food supply.

1961

The flood of refugees to West Berlin reaches its peak. The SED responds on 13 August by erecting the Berlin Wall. The order is given to open fire on those escaping. The first deaths follow.

1962

Peter Fechter is shot trying to climb the Berlin Wall and bleeds to death.

National military service is introduced in the DDR.

1963

The sixth SED Party Conference announces economic reforms and liberalization in cultural and youth policy.

1964

The FDJ jamboree marks the launch of a new and more open youth policy. The music and more relaxed style of the new radio station DT 64 wins a large audience.

The Trabant 601 enters production.

1965

The Central Committee reverses many cultural reforms. Critical films, books and plays as well as all beat music are banned.

Women are granted free access to the »Planned Child Pill«.

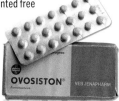

1966

Ban of the DEFA-Film »Spur der Steine«.

The foundation of what was to become the »Oktoberklub« leads to the emergence of the FDJ folk movement.

1968

DDR involvement in Warsaw Pact invasion of Czechoslovakia and the suppression of the Prague Spring. The role of the NVA is restricted to bringing up the rear.

1969

A rumour spreads that the Rolling Stones are to play a concert in the Springer house in West Berlin. Beat fans travel to East Berlin in the hope of hearing them – mingling with the crowds celebrating the twentieth anniversary of the DDR.

W.eltfestspiele
der Jugend
und Studenten

Berlin   1973
Hauptstadt der DDR

1970

During Willy Brandt's visit to Erfurt, the crowd breaks through the cordon to cheer underneath his hotel window. The event shows the dangers of détente for the SED.

1971

Erich Honecker suc- ceeds Walter Ulbricht as the leader of the SED. He reverses Ulbricht's econom- ic reforms and an- nounces the »Uni- ty of Economic and Social Policy«. This involves spending on social policy financed by borrowing and the curtailment of productive economic investment.

The Four Power Agreement guarantees the status of West Berlin.

1972

The Olympic Games at Munich sees the first participation by the DDR in a summer Olympics. The Basic Treaty establishes re- lations between the DDR and West Germany.

Abortion is legalized in the DDR.

1973

The tenth World Festival of Youth in East Berlin. The SED liberalizes its youth policy. Walter Ulbricht dies during the celebrations.

Both German states join the UN.

Launch of the housing programme.

1974

Jürgen Sparwasser scores the winning goal against West Germany at the Football World Cup. West Germany still goes on to win the World Cup.

1975
The DDR and West Germany sign the »Helsinki Accords«.

1976
New social measures bring young families with children a range of advantages.

Introduction of the 40-hour week.

The expulsion of singer-songwriter Wolf Biermann sparks protest from prominent artists.

1977
Rising coffee prices leads to the development in the DDR of a replacement coffee mix for use by companies and restaurants. The retail price of coffee is raised; protests force a U-turn.

1978
The East German cosmonaut Sigmund Jähn is the »first German in space«.

Pre-military training is introduced in schools.

1979
A period of very cold winter in December and January leads to a two-day fuel crisis and disruption to public life. Forum cheques are launched for DDR citizens, to be redeemed in Intershops.

1982
The independent peace movement finds support for its appeal for »Peace without Weapons«.

1983
West German guarantees enable the DDR to borrow billions of Marks on the international capital markets. The DDR removes its automatic guns on the inner-German border in return.

1984
A further multi-billion Mark loan is arranged for the DDR. The DDR allows a large number of East Germans to emigrate.

1985
Mikhail Gorbachev is elected to the Party Leadership in the USSR.

1986

Erich Honecker is at the height of his power at the tenth SED Party Conference, yet ever-more signs (including a fuel crisis) point to a mounting crisis.

An explosion on 26 April at the Chernobyl nuclear-power plant in Ukraine causes an atomic crisis.

Oil shortages result in a record output of brown coal.

1987

The DDR celebrates the 750th anniversary of the foundation of the city of Berlin. Improving the supply situation to »showcase« Berlin leads to dissent in the provinces.

Gorbachev announces extensive reforms in the Soviet Union (Glasnost and Perestroika) which are resisted in East Germany by the SED.

1988

Civil rights activists demonstrate for freedom of speech and travel on the fringes of an official demonstration. This provokes a wave of arrests and expulsions from the DDR.

The rock band »Silly« record their album »February« in West Berlin.

The Soviet German-language magazine »Sputnik« is banned in the DDR.

1989

East German citizens occupy the West German embassies in Budapest and Prague. Waves of refugees arrive in West Germany. Those staying in the DDR establish opposition parties. The Police use violence to disperse a demonstration on 7 October. The Leipzig »Monday Demonstration« on 9 October and that in Berlin on 4 November pass off peacefully.

The Berlin Wall falls on 9 November. The government is forced to hold round table talks with all oppositional groups.

1990

The dissolution of the Stasi.

The first free and fair elections on 18 March; the conservative CDU win a large majority.

Introduction of the D-Mark on 1 July results in the first economic dislocation in the DDR. Many DDR products are not competitive and large-scale unemployment results.

German reunification on 3 October.

BIBLIOGRAPHY

p. 24: Stefan Wolle: Die heile Welt der Diktatur. Herrschaft und Alltag in der DDR 1971-1989, Berlin ³2013, p. 303; **p. 42:** Sozialreport '90. Daten und Fakten zur sozialen Lage in der DDR, ed. by Gunnar Winkler, Berlin 1990, p. 115-118; **p. 49:** Sozialreport '90. Daten und Fakten zur sozialen Lage in der DDR, ed. by Gunnar Winkler, Berlin 1990, p. 52; Sozialreport '90. Daten und Fakten zur sozialen Lage in der DDR, ed. by Gunnar Winkler, Berlin 1990, p. 65; Sozialreport '90. Daten und Fakten zur sozialen Lage in der DDR, ed. by Gunnar Winkler, Berlin 1990, p. 49; **p. 53:** Statistisches Jahrbuch der Deutschen Demokratischen Republik, ed. by Statistisches Amt der DDR, Berlin 1990, p. 302; **p. 57:** Official Website of the IOC (International Olympic Committee), https://www.olympic.org; Statistisches Jahrbuch der Deutschen Demokratischen Republik '90, ed. by Statistisches Amt der DDR, Berlin 1990, p. 362; **pp. 60/61:** Statistisches Jahrbuch der Deutschen Demokratischen Republik '90, ed. by Statistisches Amt der DDR, Berlin 1990, S. 367; **p. 77:** Statistisches Jahrbuch der Deutschen Demokratischen Republik 1955, ed. by Staatliche Zentralverwaltung für Statistik, Berlin (DDR) 1955, p. 33; Statistisches Jahrbuch der Deutschen Demokratischen Republik '90, ed. by Statistisches Amt der DDR, Berlin 1990, S. 451; **pp. 84/85:** Sozialreport '90. Daten und Fakten zur sozialen Lage in der DDR, ed. by Gunnar Winkler, Berlin 1990, p. 285, p. 287 and p. 297f.; **p. 112:** Angela Schmole: Abteilung 26. Telefonkontrolle, Abhörmaßnahmen und Videoüberwachung (MfS-Handbuch), ed. by BStU, Berlin 2009, p. 57; **p. 123:** Bernd Lindner: »Dein Päckchen nach drüben«. Der deutsch-deutsche Paketversand und seine Rahmenbedingungen, in: Das Westpaket. Geschenksendung, keine Handelsware, ed. by Christian Härtel/Petra Kabus, Berlin 2000, pp. 25-44, p. 37; **p. 125:** Bernd Eisenfeld: Die Ausreisebewegung – eine Erscheinungsform widerständigen Verhaltens, in: Zwischen Selbstbehauptung und Anpassung: Formen des Widerstandes und der Opposition in der DDR, ed. by Ulrike Poppe/Rainer Eckert/Ilko-Sascha Kowalczuk, Berlin 1996, pp. 192-223; **p. 137:** Institut für Erhaltung und Modernisierung von Bauwerken e.V.: Sanierungsgrundlagen Plattenbau. Wohnbauten in Fertigteilbauweise (Baujahre 1958-1990). Übersicht, Berlin ²1996, p. 4; **p. 142:** Sozialreport '90. Daten und Fakten zur sozialen Lage in der DDR, ed. by Gunnar Winkler, Berlin 1990, p. 211; **p. 156:** Gislinde Schwarz: »Wenn Mutti früh zur Arbeit geht ...«. Mütter und Berufskarrieren, in: »Wenn Mutti früh zur Arbeit geht ...«. Zur Geschichte des Kindergartens in der DDR, ed. by Monika Müller-Rieger, Berlin 1997, pp. 53-74; **p. 157:** »Die Frau in der DDR«. Statistische Kennziffersammlung, Berlin 1989, in: BArch, DC 20/22686; **pp. 158/159:** Statistisches Jahrbuch der DDR, ed. by Staatliche Zentralverwaltung für Statistik, Berlin 1986, p. 282; Statistisches Jahrbuch für die Bundesrepublik Deutschland, ed. by Statistisches Bundesamt, Stuttgart/Mainz 1968, 1975 and 1985, p. 479, p. 494 and p. 464; MONICA-Survey 1983/84, cited by Christine Thiel/Dieter Johnsen: Ernährungserhebungen im Rahmen von »MONICA«, in: BFE-Bericht: Berichte der Bundesforschungsanstalt für Ernährung (Band: BFER-93-02), Bonn 1993, pp. 83-95. Ergebnisse des NUSTO, cited by G. B. M. Mensink/T. Lampert/E. Bergmann: Übergewicht und Adipositas in Deutschland 1984-2003, in: Bundesgesundheitsbl – Gesundheitsforsch – Gesundheitsschutz (48) 2005, pp. 1348-1356; **p. 160:** Sozialreport '90. Daten und Fakten zur sozialen Lage in der DDR, ed. by Gunnar Winkler, Berlin 1990, p. 203; **p. 169:** Frauenreport '90, ed. by Gunnar Winkler, Berlin 1990, p. 109; Frauenreport '90, ed. by Gunnar Winkler, Berlin 1990, p. 25; Statistisches Bundesamt, www.destatis.de.

PHOTO CREDITS

All photographs, maps and illustrations have been taken from the archive of the DDR Museum unless otherwise stated.

p. 8: BArch, Bild 183-S88796, Zühlsdorf, Erich; **p. 9:** BArch, B 145 Bild-00103642, Siegmann; BArch, Bild 183-K0616-0001-116, Junge, Heinz; **pp. 10/11:** © ddrbildarchiv.de, Rother; **p. 11:** Wolfgang Sünderhauf/Umbruch Bildarchiv; **pp. 12/13:** BArch, Bild 183-Z0513-020, Schindler, Karl-Heinz; BArch, Bild 183-U1007-003, Häßler, Ulrich; **pp. 14/15:** © SLUB/Deutsche Fotothek/Gerig, Uwe; **pp. 18/19:** BArch, Bild 183-1989-0513-042, Roeske, Robert; **pp. 22/23:** BArch, Bild 183-K1029-407, Link; **pp. 28/29:** Archiv Thüringer Allgemeine, Langner, Heinz; **p. 32:** © SLUB, Deutsche Fotothek, Weber, Gerhard; **p. 33:** BArch, Bild 183-P1212-0017, Demme, Dieter; **pp. 34/35:** BArch, Bild 183-J1126-0024-001, Siebahn, Manfred; **pp. 36/37:** © ddrbildarchiv.de, Winkler; **pp. 40/41:** BArch, Bild 183-U0705-0309, Zimmermann, Peter; **p. 41:** © ddrbildarchiv.de, Uhlenhut, Manfred; **pp. 46/47:** BArch, Bild 183-1985-1112-001, Kämper, Andreas; **p. 50:** BArch, Bild 183-W0219-0024, Uhlemann, Thomas; **p. 51:** BArch, Bild 183-1982-0120-018, Settnik, Bernd; **p. 55:** BArch, Bild 183-66400-0142, Zastrom; **p. 57:** BArch, Bild 183-1989-0513-042, Roeske, Robert; **p. 60:** BArch, Bild 183-1988-0706-418, Sindermann, Jürgen; **pp. 62/63:** BArch, Bild 183-1985-0829-070, Mittelstädt, Rainer; **p. 66:** BArch, Bild 183-1986-0417-414, Franke, Klaus; **p. 67:** © ullstein bild, Kontributor; **p. 68:** BArch, Plak 103-008-002; BArch, Bild 183-W0910-305; **p. 69:** BArch, Bild 183-K0614-0006-003, Thieme, Wolfgang; **pp. 70/71:** © ddrbildarchiv.de/Morgenstern, Klaus; Illustration © Eugenio Hansen, OFS; **pp. 72/73:** BArch, Bild 183-K1010-0007, Thieme, Wolfgang; **p. 76:** © picture alliance/Roland Holschneider; **p. 79:** BArch, B 145 Bild-00014227, Richter, Evelyn; **p. 80:** BArch, B 145 Bild-00203065, Perlia-Archiv; **p. 81:** BArch, Bild 183-1989-1201-046, Grubitzsch (geb. Raphael), Waltraud; BArch, Bild 183-1989-1106-023, Gahlbeck, Friedrich; **pp. 82/83:** BArch, Bild 183-1989-0507-005, Uhlemann, Thomas; **p. 90:** BArch, Bild 183-1984-0927-016, Müller; **p. 91:** BArch, Bild 183-P0901-101, Siebahn, Manfred; **p. 92:** BArch, Bild 183-Z0710-300, Lehmann, Thomas; BArch, Bild 183-1988-0415-401, Weisflog, Rainer; **p. 93:** BArch, Bild 183-T0829-423, Link, Hubert; **pp. 94/95:** BArch, Bild 183-1989-1218-003, Weisflog, Rainer; **p. 96/97:** BArch, Bild 183-R67154; **p. 106:** Robert-Havemann-Gesellschaft, Müller, Gerhard; **p. 107:** BArch, Bild 183-P0523-0028, Gahlbeck, Friedrich; **pp. 108/109:** BArch, Bild 183-1985-0829-070, Mittelstädt, Rainer; **pp. 110/111:** BStU, MfS, HA III, DI 0011, Fo, Nr. 0009; **pp. 118/119:** © Arthur Schmidt/Gvoon; **pp. 120/121:** © Harald Schmitt; **p. 125:** Günther Mach, Sammlungsbestand Gedenkstätte Deutsche Teilung Marienborn; **pp. 126/127:** © Harald Schmitt; **p. 130:** © SLUB/Deutsche Fotothek/Danigel, Gerd; **p. 131:** BArch, Bild 183-N0920-302, Junge, Heinz; BArch, Bild 183-66606-0004, Stöhr; **pp. 132/133:** © SLUB/Deutsche Fotothek/Weber, Gerhard; **p. 134:** BArch, Bild 183-W0204-0013, Schindler, Karl-Heinz; **p. 135:** BArch, Bild 183-R1231-0017, Bartocha, Benno; **p. 141:** © ddrbildarchiv.de/Uhlenhut, Manfred; **p. 143:** BArch, Bild 183-Z1007-023, Kasper, Jan Peter; © SLUB/Deutsche Fotothek/Weber, Gerhard; **pp. 144/145:** © Deutsche Fotothek/Danigel, Gerd; **p. 154:** © ddr-bildarchiv.de, Archiv 1; **p. 154:** BArch, Bild 183-Z0331-001, Thieme, Wolfgang; **pp. 160/161:** BArch, Bild 183-1986-1209-014, Ritter, Steffen; **pp. 164/165:** BArch, Bild 183-E0905-0034-001, Hochneder, Christa; **pp. 166/167:** BArch, Bild 183-L0902-114, Häßler, Ulrich; **p. 168:** © Harald Schmitt; **pp. 172/173:** © Werner Klemke; **pp. 174/175:** © Harald Schmitt; **p. 178:** Heinz Lutz/Archiv Peter Kurze Bremen; **p. 179:** © ddrbildarchiv.de/Uhlenhut, Manfred; **pp. 180/181:** © Sigrid Marotz; **pp. 184/185:** Verlag Peter Kurze, Bremen; **pp. 186/187:** © Sigrid Marotz; **p. 188:** © Sigrid Marotz; **p. 189:** © ullstein bild; **p. 192:** Bpk, Bild-Nr.: 30021050; BArch, B 285 Plak-008-002; Bpk, Bild-Nr.: 30013941; **p. 193:** BArch, B 145 Bild-F005191-0040A; BArch, Bild 183-29617-0002, Sturm, Horst; BArch, **p. 194:** BArch, Bild 183-91036-0001, Krisch, Werner; BArch, Bild 183-F0321-0204-001, Franke, Klaus; © SLUB/Deutsche Fotothek/Hermann, Manfred; **p. 195:** © Max Scheler Estate/Agentur Focus/Scheler, Max; BArch, Plak 102-063-007, Bertram, Axel; BArch, Bild 183-N1210-0312, Gahlbeck, Friedrich; **p. 196:** BArch, Bild 183-1990-0226-301, Mittelstädt, Rainer; **p. 197:** BArch, Bild 183-1990-0226-301, Mittelstädt, Rainer; **p. 198:** BArch, Bild 183-1990-0329-029, Gahlbeck, Friedrich.

GERMAN DEMOCRATIC REPUBLIC

IN EUROPE

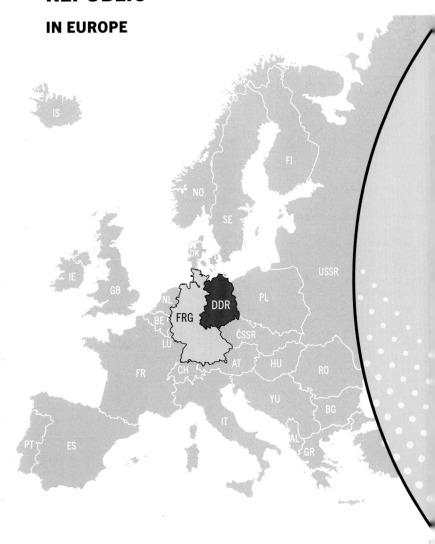